FROM THE WORLD'S
TOP KOSHER RESTAURANTS

SECRET
RESTAURANT
RECIPES

Food Stylist **AMIT FARBER**
Photography **DANIEL LAILAH**
Design **RACHELADLERDESIGN.COM**
Publisher **MESORAH PUBLICATIONS,** LTD.

Published by **ARTSCROLL / SHAAR PRESS**
4401 Second Avenue / Brooklyn, NY 11232 / (718) 921-9000
www.artscroll.com

Distributed in Israel by **SIFRIATI / A. GITLER**
Moshav Magshimim / Israel

Distributed in Europe by **LEHMANNS**
Unit E, Viking Business Park, Rolling Mill Road
Jarrow, Tyne and Wear, NE32 3DP / England

Distributed in Australia and New Zealand by
GOLDS WORLD OF JUDAICA
3-13 William Street / Balaclava, Melbourne 3183, Victoria / Australia

Distributed in South Africa by **KOLLEL BOOKSHOP**
Northfield Centre / 17 Northfield Avenue / Glenhazel 2192 /
Johannesburg, South Africa

ISBN-10: 1-4226-1528-6 / ISBN-13: 978-1-4226-1528-7
Printed by Noble Book Press

WITH THANKS TO

HASHEM

The Source of all our strength.

THE SCHAPIRA FAMILY

Sharing the food with all of you makes it all the more delicious.

PARENTS, IN-LAWS, AND THE EXTENDED SCHAPIRA & ROTH FAMILIES //
There are a lot of you. And lots of opinions. But all those opinions and recommendations (and photos of each restaurant meal you enjoyed), are what helped make this book so great. -L.

THE DWEK FAMILY

AVI & KIDS //
The first reason I cook is to make you happy. The anticipation of your joy is my pleasure in the process.

PARENTS, IN-LAWS, AND THE EXTENDED DWEK & MATALON FAMILIES //
My favorite thing to do in the world is prepare for the times I have you around my table. Guests coming = my excitement. -V.

THE CREATIVE TEAM

RACHEL ADLER // Designer
Brilliance is your design.

DANIEL LAILAH // Photographer
The master of light.

AMIT FARBER // Stylist
Finding magic and beauty in every dish.

RENEE MULLER // Prop Stylist
Your impeccable taste, transported to our pages.

THE ARTSCROLL TEAM

RABBI MEIR ZLOTOWITZ & GEDALIAH ZLOTOWITZ // The Publishers
For the confidence in this momentous project.

FELICE EISNER // Editor
Our mistakes, your joy. No more mistakes, more joy.

MIRIAM PASCAL // PR & Marketing
Bringing the passion to the people.

DEVORAH BLOCH // Graphics
Crossing the finish line and off to print.

TOVA OVITS & JUDI DICK //
Proofreading
Keeping the i dotted and the t crossed.

MORE

ZALMAN ROTH & TZVI ADLER // Europe and Israel Correspondents
We sleep while you work to make this an international book.

MARNIE LEVY, SINA MIZRAHI, JENINE SHWEKEY, MELINDA STRAUSS & SHOSHY TURIN // Restaurant Connossieurs
We made you tell us about every meal.

SET YOUR TABLE & THE TABLE BY C.S. THAU // Props
Thanks for the best from your shelves.

CHEFS & OWNERS OF THE WORLD'S TOP KOSHER RESTAURANTS

We salute and appreciate the work you do every day.

THE RECIPES

LOTS OF PEOPLE ASK US, "HOW DID YOU TWO MEET?"

INTRODUCTION

A few years ago, Victoria was writing an article about bread mixers. After making many batches of dough using every type of machine (and her hands), she interviewed food personalities to learn how they knead their dough. And so, Leah and Victoria's first-ever conversation was about the Bosch kitchen machine.

We both then discovered that we like food, we love to learn, and we share the same obsessiveness with sharing what we learn.

WE BOTH FEEL THE NEED TO BANISH BORING DINNERS.

And that made the perfect partnership for cookbook co-writers.

We have different backgrounds and different taste buds, which broadened our perspectives. We had only one thing in common in our culinary upbringing: family nights at Chinese restaurants.

In Leah's childhood home, popular dishes included classic Ashkenaz fare such as kugels, chicken soup, eggs and liver, and of course, babka. Dinners were more diverse, with homemade pizza or veal chops (never meatballs and spaghetti), and influences from Israel such as falafel and shnitzel (the Thursday-night meal). Victoria's favorite Thursday-night dish was her mom's keskesoon, a traditional Syrian dish made with Israeli couscous, fried onions, and chickpeas. She'd enjoy it with sour cream. The attitude toward food in Deal, though, was super health-conscious. Victoria doesn't remember eating French fries while growing up, but there was always salad on the table. When one of her brothers came home with a coconut, Victoria watched the Jamaican housekeeper shred and fry it. Mistake. In Victoria's house, the only thing that was meant to be fried was the kibbe.

AS FOOD WRITERS, WHEN HOME COOKS ASK FOR ADVICE, WE TELL THEM

"Try lots of new recipes."

You'll learn something new, whether it's a technique or flavor pairing, with each new recipe you try. *Reading about food opens up a world; getting into the kitchen reinforces it.*

We both spent the last couple of years focusing on creating the

MADE EASY

series of cookbooks, including *Passover Made Easy, Starters & Sides Made Easy, Kids Cooking Made Easy*, and *Dairy Made Easy*.

When we wrote these books, we knew that being home cooks worked to our advantage. We understand the types of recipes other kosher cooks, just like us, need. We understand your lifestyle, your pantries, and your time constraints.

Our **MADE EASY** books present the dishes for everyday cooks. Cooking, for us, is fun, and we want it to be fun for you too. It shouldn't be intimidating to get really great food to the table. And we understand it, because, as mothers of growing families, we live it.

AND AS MUCH AS WE LOVE OUR HOME COOKING, WE ALSO LOVE GOING OUT TO RESTAURANTS.

Everyone — even those most devoted to the kitchen — enjoys the atmosphere and the experience of dining out. But for many of us, restaurants give us an opportunity to try dishes we might not have thought to prepare on our own.

There is a food revolution in the kosher world, and while we're all bringing new and interesting dishes to the table,

WE NEED TO GIVE CREDIT TO THE PEOPLE WHO

BROUGHT US ALL THESE NEW FLAVORS WE'RE EXPERIENCING: KOSHER CHEFS.

They don't speak loudly; they're often in the "back of the house." But, probably every time we eat out, we bring their influences back home to our tables. How often do you enjoy something in a restaurant and then go home to try to duplicate it?

SECRET RESTAURANT RECIPES

further transports that restaurant experience to your home kitchen.

We weren't satisfied with relaxing while enjoying the food they served. We needed to learn their secrets. We spent a year picking the brains of the world's best

OUR TEACHERS WERE THE TOP KOSHER CHEFS FROM AROUND THE WORLD.

kosher chefs. So, now that we've been privy to go behind the scenes at top kosher restaurants, what did we learn?

The best secret ingredients are simply the best quality ingredients. And while we discovered lots of secret recipes, our biggest prizes were when we also learned a new technique. And while we did add a few ingredients to our pantries (you'll learn about them on page 14), there were only two or three ingredients in the whole book that were only available commercially and needed substitutions.

Besides reducing recipes with yields of 5 gallons to servings for 4, the only adjustment needed to adapt these recipes for the home cook was in the cooking times. Restaurant ovens and fires are simply hotter and more intense. Meat that cooks in 4 minutes at a restaurant is definitely still going to be rare in your own oven. Our #1 lesson was the importance of a hot pan (see page 9).

NOT EVERY CHEF WRITES DOWN RECIPES OR EVEN BELIEVES IN RECIPES.

To attain some recipes, we had to go back into the restaurant kitchens and watch them being prepared. Perhaps that's when we learned the most.

We didn't eat in every single restaurant, but we did network to get personal recommendations on each one.

Some recipes might seem a bit more involved. Restaurants do cook fresh and serve quickly, though. We saw how they prep most components in advance, and assemble others fresh to order, making it easier to bring a great meal to the table. We brought these tips to our kitchens as well, keeping a stock of items like salad dressings or fresh roasted peppers.

This book isn't only for the nights when you want recreate that dinner for two at home. Restaurants also mean family time, so there are lots of family-friendly options too. And of course, we also bring restaurant inspiration to our Shabbat and holiday meals, and more.

After completing this book, we have new appreciation for the people who serve us food on the days we want a night off from cooking.

LEAH & VICTORIA

TECHNIQUES

WATCH THAT PAN

If you walk into the "back of the house" (the kitchen) at any restaurant, you'll find empty pans sitting over open flames. This way, when the orders come in, the pan is ready for use. Add the oil (sizzle), then the meat/chicken/fish/veggies (whatever is being cooked … sizzle again). A hot pan is essential for creating that dark crust on proteins and for properly sautéing veggies.

At home, mostly because we're impatient, we often make the mistake of not waiting until our pan is hot enough (that's also why the food sticks to the pan). And while we don't recommend keeping pans over open flames in your home kitchen … the solution we can offer is to have patience with the pans.

This technique is used in most recipes throughout this book, and is especially important when cooking proteins.

JUDGING A RESTAURANT BY THE FRIES

Fine dining, fast food. Dairy, meat, fish. It doesn't matter what else is on the menu. There's one thing that all restaurants have in common. And that's the French fries.

Any good restaurant must have great fries. But how do they do it?

Begin by cutting your potatoes into fries. Then soak your fries in ice-cold salted water, for at least 30 minutes or up to overnight. Dry completely.

Season French fries when they're hot so the seasoning sticks. Season with kosher salt or table salt (sea salt won't stick). Our chefs also use: coarse black pepper, Cajun spice (see page 205), Parmesan cheese (see page 48), a sprinkle of truffle oil, or chopped fresh herbs.

The most commonly used French-fry potato is Idaho (some use red potatoes, and others use the specialty Kennebec).

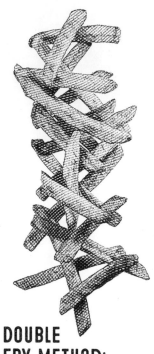

DOUBLE FRY METHOD:

Heat oil to 300°F-325°F. Add fries and fry until they turn a light blonde color. Let drain and cool completely on a wire rack. Heat oil to 350°F-375°F and fry until golden.

BLANCH AND FRY METHOD:

Blanch French fries in salted boiling water until tender. (Fries that are blanched first absorb less oil.) Drain and let cool. Heat oil to 350°F and fry until golden.

EGGS + CREAM = USUALLY GREAT TOGETHER

It just depends how you do it. If you were to add egg yolks into a simmering cream, you'd have scrambled eggs. Sure, they'd be a very delicious scramble, but we don't think that's what you were aiming for. To keep eggs from curdling, they need to be tempered. While whisking constantly, pour a little of the hot liquid into the eggs. Continue whisking while adding hot liquid, a little at a time, allowing the temperature of the eggs to rise very slowly.

This technique is used in the following recipes:

THIN CRUST PIZZA

If you're a fan of thin, crispy crust, we have something in common. But thin crust can also get weighed down and soggy when there's too much sauce. Solutions? We have a few. Place a layer of cheese first, then top with spoons of sauce. You can also try baking the crust for a few minutes before adding toppings, or brushing on a thin layer of your sauce using a pastry brush.

This technique is used in the following recipe:

Pizza de Nonna, page 233.

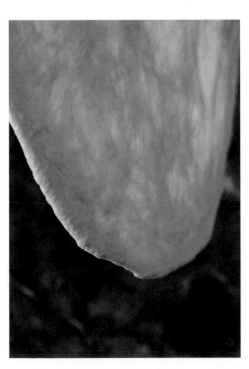

EMULSIFY

Think oil and water can't get along? They can in an emulsion, as long as you give them time to get to know each other. When making mayonnaise or a vinaigrette (both of which include water-based liquids and oil), after combining all the ingredients except the oil, whisk in that oil very slowly, all while mixing or blending. To keep the oil and water from separating again, the mixture needs to include an emulsifier, such as the egg in the mayonnaise (which contains the emulsifier lecithin). Mustard and honey also have emulsifying agents, making them worthy additions to your salad dressing.

This technique is used in the following recipes:

Most salad dressings, but especially the Caesar Salad, page 87.

Basil Fries, page 48.

PLASTIC WRAP IN THE OVEN? NO WAY ?!? YES!

The secret to succulent ribs and other meats is to wrap the pan with plastic wrap — just make sure to cover the plastic wrap in aluminum foil so it's not directly exposed to the heat (exposed plastic will melt and burn). The plastic wrap helps keep all the steam inside, keeping the contents of the pan very moist. You can also use this trick to keep reheated food from drying out.

This technique is used in the following recipe:

Braised Short Ribs, page 156.

COATING THE BACK OF A SPOON

This term can be confusing. Lots of recipes that include sauces and custards call for cooking the mixture until it thickens enough to coat the back of a spoon. But the sauce seems to coat the back of the spoon from the very beginning … so how do we know when it's ready?

To determine when the sauce has really "coated the back of a spoon," swipe your finger across the back of that famous spoon. If the sauce runs, it's not yet ready. When you swipe your finger and the line stays in place, you're good to go.

This technique is used in the following recipes:

Chef's Special, page 164.

Cereal Milk Ice Cream, page 276.

PERKY HERBS

We love coming home from the supermarket with a bunch of fresh basil, looking forward to smelling (and using) the herbs all week long. Unfortunately, those leaves don't look so fresh and tempting after a day of hanging out in the fridge. So, how did we bring our greens to life so they could look bright and perky in the photographs?

To shock herbs back to their former green life, remove the bruised leaves and soak the rest in an ice bath for a few minutes. Basil will take just a couple of minutes, but stronger herbs, such as parsley and cilantro, will take longer, about 15 minutes. Dry thoroughly and your pretty leaves are again ready for use.

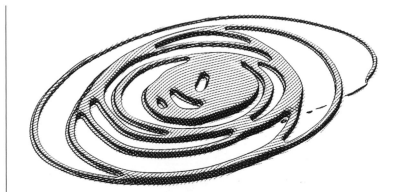

GOOD THINGS START WITH CARAMEL

When we saw that Café Rimon's teriyaki sauce begins by caramelizing sugar, we thought, "Oh … wow." There are vanilla fans and chocolate fans … but caramel is the kind of thing everyone agrees on. Caramel is simply melted sugar, but how do we get there?

When you add sugar to your pan over low-medium heat, you'll need to give it your full, undivided attention. It doesn't mean you need to keep playing with it. You need to stir only when you see sugar melting (usually around the edges) to keep the whole pan cooking evenly and prevent one spot from burning.

You will need to stir a lot, but if you start to get sugar rocks instead of caramel, it means you've stirred too much. Let it sit until the melting begins again, then stir gently until your sugar is liquefied and golden.

This technique is used in the following recipe:

Salmon & Tuna with Teriyaki Sauce, page 194.

THE SECRET PANTRY

SAN MARZANO WHOLE PEELED TOMATOES

Are they better than your standard canned tomatoes? Lots of chefs think so. San Marzano tomatoes are elongated plum tomatoes and have fewer seeds and more sweetness than other tomatoes. Today, not all San Marzano tomatoes come from the San Marzano region of Italy, as the seeds are also used in domestic crops. *(Note: Not all Cento San Marzano tomatoes, pictured, are kosher certified).*

Every chef will give credit for a great dish to the great ingredients, the foremost being fresh, in-season produce. And while there are lots of "secret" ingredients that contribute to great dishes, here are a few you might want to know more about.

CHEF KNIFE

Every chef's #1 kitchen tool. For more on our chefs' favorite knives, see pages 25 and 117.

TRUFFLE OIL Chefs have a love/hate relationship with truffle oil. When used correctly (e.g., in Basil Fries, page 48), it can be a magical ingredient. Although most versions don't contain actual truffles (the base is usually olive or grapeseed oil infused with the truffle aroma), the oil gives dishes an earthy, multidimensional flavor.

WILDFLOWER HONEY Wildflower Honey is made by bees collecting pollen from random wildflowers. It has a more robust flavor and is a bit darker than regular honey (which can be used as a substitute), and is amazing in the Heirloom Tomato Salad (page 102).

DIGITAL SCALE *A kitchen must! Digital food scales aren't just for dieters. Most restaurant kitchens measure ingredients more accurately by weight instead of by volume for consistent results, especially when baking (see Financiers, page 250).*

DRIED PORCINI MUSHROOMS & PORCINI MUSHROOM POWDER

The flavor of the porcini mushroom is enhanced when it's dried (much like a sun-dried tomato); the mushrooms are a rich addition to sauces and stews. And while kosher-certified dried porcini mushrooms are readily available, you will have to shop online to find porcini mushroom powder (add it to flour when breading proteins, as in the Chef's Special on page 164, or add it to sauces and soups, as in the Bolognese on page 182). We made our own powder by pulsing our dried porcini mushrooms in a food processor and then grinding them into powder using the coffee grinder. Try it—then you'll have a nice supply to keep on your spice rack, ready to use.

DINNER

FOR TWO
MEAT

STARTER

Ahi Tuna Two Ways
(page 26)

OR

House Salad
(page 94)

MAIN

Chef's Special
(page 164)

OR

Côte de Beouf
(page 168)

OR

Duck with
Sour Cherry Reduction
(page 152)

SIDE

Popover Potatoes
(page 52)

DESSERT

Pareve Crème Brûlée
(page 258)

DINNER

FOR TWO
DAIRY

STARTER

Portobello
Mushroom Soup
(page 76)

SALAD

Rockport Salad
(page 118)

MAIN

Fettuccine
Tri Funghi
(page 230)

OR

Salmon & Tuna
with Teriyaki Sauce
(page 194)

OR

Miso-Tomato Sea Bass
(page 210)

DESSERT

Financiers
with Whipped Cream
& Fresh Berries
(page 250)

STARTERS & SIDES

"IN A RESTAURANT CHOOSE A TABLE NEAR A WAITER."
~Jewish Proverb

MUSHROOM DROPS

ORCHIDËA

OWNER/CHEF
Owners Ofer Kohen and Mazal Werczberger

LOCATION
In the Borough Park neighborhood of Brooklyn, New York

So how did we convince restaurant chefs and owners to give us recipes? In this case, it was helpful that co-owner Ofer Kohen practically watched me grow up. When he was younger, he worked at a pizzeria around the corner from my house. For close to a decade, I'd stop there every Friday for pizza (it was one of the only foods I ate back then). Orchidëa opened just in time for my taste buds to grow up.

At Orchidëa, every dish, beginning with the bread on the table and ending with the chocolate soufflé, is freshly made — and I taste the difference. From the classics (Penne alla Vodka; Cheese Ravioli; Chilean Sea Bass, Napoleon, and Tiramisu) to the new dishes (Penne Roma, Coconut Tilapia, Coral Salad), all are consistently fabulous.

It's befitting that the first recipe in this book is also one of the first recipes we received. **-L.**

MUSHROOM DROPS

YIELD *18-20 drops*

CATEGORY *dairy*

DESCRIPTION

Mushrooms in a pastry bundle over chopped tomato cream

We asked co-owner Mazal Werczberger why she decided to open a restaurant. She said, "I used to make unusually good schnitzel and Yemenite soup. Everyone would tell me I should open a restaurant." Why a dairy restaurant then? "I still don't know."

INGREDIENTS

3 TBSP	oil
1 LARGE	sweet onion, *finely diced*
4	garlic cloves, *crushed*
1 LB	white button mushrooms, *finely diced*
1 TSP	kosher salt
•	pinch coarse black pepper
6-8	sheets phyllo dough OR feuille de brick

SAUCE:

2 TBSP	oil
1 SMALL	onion, *diced*
1 LARGE	tomato, *diced*
2	garlic cloves
½ CUP	marinara sauce
1 TSP	pareve consommé powder
½ TSP	kosher salt
•	pinch coarse black pepper
5 TBSP	heavy cream

INSTRUCTIONS

1. Heat oil in a sauté pan over medium heat. Add onion and sauté for 5-6 minutes. Add garlic and mushrooms; sauté until mushrooms are dark brown and liquid has evaporated, about 20 minutes. Season with salt and pepper.

2. Preheat oven to 350°F. Line a baking sheet with parchment paper. Spray parchment paper with nonstick cooking spray.

3. Place phyllo dough in 2 stacks of 3-4 sheets each. Slice into 4-inch squares. Turn two of the sheets on each square so that the square now resembles a star. Spray the corners with nonstick cooking spray. Place a heaping teaspoon of mushroom filling in the center of each star. Bring the corners up like a bundle, pinch together, and twist. Place on prepared baking sheet. Spray with nonstick cooking spray. Bake until golden, about 8-10 minutes.

4. Meanwhile, prepare the sauce: Heat oil in a sauté pan over medium heat. Add onion and sauté for 4-5 minutes. Add tomato and garlic and cook for 20 minutes. Stir in marinara sauce, consommé powder, salt, pepper, and heavy cream. Cook until warmed through.

5. To serve, spread a large spoonful of sauce across the plate and top with 3 mushroom drops.

CLOSER LOOK *We tested these drops using phyllo dough, which works fine, but the restaurant uses a slightly thicker pastry dough called feuille de brick (also spelled brik or brique). Feuille de brick is more widely available commercially. While both phyllo and feuille de brick can be baked, the latter can also be fried (when frying, spring roll wrappers make the optimal substitution).*

Here's an easy garnish idea: Top your mushroom drops with spiralized raw beets (you'll need a spiralizer to copy them exactly as shown).

These drops freeze well. At Orchidëa, they're frozen after assembling and baked fresh to order.

GUACAMOLE AND CHIPS

 Glatt·A·LaCarte

GLATT A LA CARTE

OWNER/CHEF
Owner Binem Naimen /
Chef Mark Green

LOCATION
In the Borough Park neighborhood of Brooklyn, New York

I asked my sister-in-law Janel, who is a regular at Glatt A La Carte, which recipe we should feature in this book. She mentioned her favorite Peanut Butter Mousse dessert and her favorite chicken entrée, but this appetizer was the pick. "Even though it's a basic, it's just so good. Almost every table orders it," she said.

In the back of the house, Chef Mark Green has become renowned for a creative, evolving menu and unique seasoning blends and sauces (so much so, that the spices and sauces are now bottled and sold commercially).

Popular dishes include the Texas Beef Spring Rolls, Chimichurri Skirt Steak, and anything from the grill, including the House Cut Boneless Ribeye, and new additions to the menu like Peppercorn-crusted Beef Filet for Two.

It's not just the food that the regulars love. Janel added, "One of the other things I love about Glatt A La Carte is that the owner comes over during or at the end of the meal to make sure we're happy and ask if we enjoyed. And he genuinely wants to hear what you'll have to say. If you go often, you'll recognize the faces of the wait staff. They're experienced and attentive … you'll always have a full glass." - **V**.

GUACAMOLE AND CHIPS

YIELD *4-6 servings*

CATEGORY *pareve*

DESCRIPTION

Guacamole served with tortilla chips and topped with pico de gallo

Over the years, Glatt A La Carte has updated the presentation of this dish. In one presentation, the chips stand up in a row in the guacamole. In another, it goes in a ramekin with the chips all around. We plated the guacamole and pico de gallo using a ring mold and stood the chips around the perimeter.

INGREDIENTS

2 LARGE	avocados
1 TBSP	finely diced red onion
1-2 TBSP	finely diced jalapeño *(1 with seeds, 1 without)*
1 TBSP	chopped fresh cilantro
1 TBSP	fresh lime juice
½ TSP	kosher salt, *or to taste*
•	pinch coarse black pepper

PICO DE GALLO:

5-6	red grape tomatoes, *halved*
5-6	yellow grape tomatoes, *halved*
1 TBSP	finely diced red onion
½ TSP	diced jalapeño, *without seeds*
1 TBSP	lime juice
½ TSP	kosher salt
•	pinch coarse black pepper

TORTILLA CHIPS:

3	*(10-in)* flour or corn tortillas, *each cut into 8 wedges*
1 CUP	vegetable oil, *for frying*
•	kosher salt, *for sprinkling*
2	cilantro sprigs, *for garnish*

INSTRUCTIONS

1 In a small bowl, mash avocado flesh with a fork, retaining some texture. Add red onion, jalapeño, and cilantro. Add lime juice, salt, and pepper. Mix gently. Taste and adjust salt and lime juice if needed. If not using immediately, cover with plastic wrap directly over guacamole and remove any air bubbles. Refrigerate.

2 Prepare the pico de gallo: In a small bowl, combine tomatoes, red onion, jalapeño, lime juice, salt, and pepper. Toss gently, cover, and marinate for 1 hour or more.

3 Prepare the tortilla chips: Heat oil in a saucepan or deep fryer to 350°F. Add tortilla wedges and fry until golden brown. Remove from oil and drain on paper towels. Sprinkle with salt.

4 To serve, top guacamole with pico de gallo. Garnish with cilantro and serve alongside tortilla chips.

TIDBIT *Most restaurants have high staff turnover. At Glatt A La Carte, the chef has been there for 14 years, since its inception; other kitchen staff have been there for a decade.*

Prepare your chips in advance, make your pico de gallo earlier in the day, and combine the guacamole ingredients close to serving time.

Chef Mark Green says a chef's three must-have tools in the kitchen are: A 9-inch chef knife, a 6-inch boning knife, and a serrated knife.

Glatt A La Carte has lots of specials that aren't always on the menu … but if you tried something once and really want it again, make a request, and they'll prepare it especially for you.

"I'm very impressed by home cooks; they care. TLC is the most important part of cooking. In Borough Park, some of the ladies — they can really cook."

— CHEF MARK GREEN, GLATT A LA CARTE

SHILOH'S
A MODERN STEAK HOUSE ®

SHILOH'S

OWNER/CHEF
Owners Fabrice & Geoffrey Ghanem / Chef Lou Lemorrocco

LOCATION

On Pico Boulevard in Los Angeles, California

While we were working on this book, even if it was late at night, Leah always wanted to figure out what else we could accomplish before calling it a day. That's when we got to appreciate the three-hour time difference between New York and Los Angeles. The East Coast might be asleep, but the West Coast was still hopping.

One of those late-night calls found us on the line with Fabrice Ghanem, with the din of the dinner crowd still buzzing in the background. When Fabrice and his brother Geoffrey, French Tunisian Jews, came to America, they envisioned an upscale French restaurant like the one their parents had run in the south of France.

Shiloh's, a French steakhouse with ivory leather tufted seating, delivers on that refined, at-your-service experience, which begins with an exceptional tapenade and continues with elegant appetizers such as this. The house-made harissa is unique, as are the five sauces you can choose to enjoy with your steak (those sauces have made Shiloh's famous and are also available nationwide, including a sweet, spicy Caribbean-style sauce).

You don't have to wait until evening to enjoy a Shiloh's meal. One of our Los Angeles friends tells us to go for lunch. "Lunch is the best … get a sandwich." I suppose that's the BBQ Brisket Sandwich … yes, with Shiloh's famous barbecue sauce. **- V.**

AHI TUNA TWO WAYS

YIELD *2 servings*

CATEGORY *pareve*

DESCRIPTION

Duo of seared sashimi and tuna tartare with avocado

At Shiloh's, garnishes include mandarin oranges, wakame (seaweed), crunchy wonton strips, with a side salad of mixed greens dressed with a sesame vinaigrette. We topped our tuna with scallion ribbons.

Not all tuna will make great tuna tartare; the taste varies greatly with the quality. Purchase sushi grade tuna only!

We placed our avocado slices against the walls of a ring mold and filled the rest of the mold with the tuna.

INGREDIENTS

5 OZ	sushi grade ahi tuna, *divided*
3 TBSP	mayonnaise
2 TBSP	soy sauce
4 TSP	sesame oil, *divided*
¼ CUP	sesame seeds
1	ripe avocado, *sliced*

GARNISH:

2 OZ	pickled ginger
1 OZ	wasabi

INSTRUCTIONS

1 Dice half the tuna into small cubes. In a small mixing bowl, combine diced tuna with mayonnaise, soy sauce, and 1 teaspoon sesame oil.

2 Roll remaining tuna in sesame seeds. Heat remaining sesame oil in a nonstick pan over medium heat. Add tuna and sear for about 1 minute on each side. Blot with a paper towel to remove excess oil; set aside to cool.

3 To serve, arrange sliced avocado on two plates. Top with diced tuna. Slice seared tuna into thin slices and arrange next to diced tuna. Garnish with ginger and wasabi.

SEA BASS SPRING ROLLS

We have lots of friends who eat out more often than we do, and they keep us posted on their favorite dishes at their favorite restaurants. One of those friends is Jenine Shwekey. I usually bump into her on Friday mornings, the day we both drive carpool. That's when I heard about Mocha Bleu, one of her favorite spots.

And that's when she excitedly told me about Mocha Bleu's Artichoke Ravioli (one of the specials), Mozzarella Puffs (fresh mozzarella cheese battered and fried), and these Sea Bass Spring Rolls (I love sea bass and Leah loves spring rolls; sounds like the perfect starter). The rest of the menu has great variety and creativity, including the tempting selection of pizzas, such as the Bruschetta Pizza and the Portofino, which emerge from Mocha Bleu's cherry wood-burning oven. There are also gluten-free pizza and pasta alternatives.

With glass-tiled walls and Lucite seating, the modern Mocha Bleu ambiance is very striking. But your eyes might wander to the macarons, tarts, and pastries housed in the glass cases of the in-house authentic French patisserie (why not return in the morning to enjoy a latte and pastry at the coffee bar?). -V.

MOCHA BLEU

MOCHA BLEU

OWNER/CHEF
Owner Naftali Abenaim

LOCATION
Teaneck, NJ

NEW JERSEY

SEA BASS SPRING ROLLS

YIELD *14 spring rolls*

CATEGORY *pareve*

DESCRIPTION

Chilean sea bass and kani mix, with Asian garlic sauce

Mirin is a Japanese rice wine, a staple in Japanese cuisine. It's the ingredient that's traditionally used to flavor sushi rice. It has a very low alcohol content and a strong, sweet flavor, so you only need a little bit.

At Mocha Bleu, these spring rolls are served alongside sweet ginger sauce for dipping. To make your own, whisk together 6 tablespoons sweet chili sauce, 2 teaspoons soy sauce, 2 teaspoons rice wine vinegar, 2 teaspoons sugar, 1 teaspoon fresh minced ginger, and 1 minced garlic clove.

This recipe is a great example of a way a home cook can stretch an expensive ingredient like sea bass.

INGREDIENTS

- ½ LB   Chilean sea bass, *cut into ¼-in cubes*
- 1 LB   kani *(imitation crab),* *shredded*
- 3 TBSP   mayonnaise
- 1 TBSP   sesame oil
- ½ TSP   mirin
- ½ TSP   kosher salt
- 14   sheets feuille de brick or spring roll wrappers
- •   oil, *for frying*

INSTRUCTIONS

1. In a medium bowl, combine sea bass, kani, mayonnaise, sesame oil, mirin, and salt.

2. Spread filling over the bottom-center of each wrapper. Fold in sides; roll up tightly.

3. Heat oil in a saucepan or deep fryer. Add spring rolls, a few at a time, and fry until golden brown, about 3-4 minutes.

DUCK SPRING ROLLS

PRIME BISTRO

OWNER/CHEF

Chef Simon Azoulay

LOCATION

Lawrence, New York

NEW YORK

Back in Casablanca, the father of Prime Bistro's owner was a butcher on a large scale, supplying fresh meat for the entire Jewish community; the owner's mother was a chef. When the family left Morocco, the business of charcuterie (the craft of preparing meat) was the natural step in continuing the family legacy.

Prime Bistro is a high-end butcher shop and French steakhouse (you'll sit on classic Thonet bistro chairs circa 1940). The meat is dry aged — wine and dine on an incredible steak or take the raw cuts home to impress your barbecue guests. (Those who work in the Central Avenue area also like to treat themselves to a steak sandwich at lunchtime.)

Prime Bistro has lots of fun appetizers to enjoy as a prelude to your classic steakhouse meal (signature steaks include the Prime Bistro Filet and the Delmonico). The Tuna Tartare is crunchy and distinctive, but the appetizer we received the most requests for were these Duck Spring Rolls, which were surprisingly simple to prepare. - **L**.

DUCK SPRING ROLLS

YIELD *20 spring rolls*

CATEGORY *meat*

DESCRIPTION

Pekin duck spring rolls with duck confit and chili hoisin sauce

Prime Bistro's owner is the former owner of The Box Tree, the beautiful restaurant housed in an art-filled Manhattan townhouse that was kosher from 2003-2005.

INGREDIENTS

4 OZ	duck breast
4 OZ	dark duck meat
3 TBSP	allspice
3 TBSP	ground star anise *(or fennel)*
6 TBSP	soy sauce
1 TBSP	brown sugar
1 TSP	rice vinegar
2 TBSP	sesame oil
¾ CUP	finely diced daikon
1¼ CUPS	chopped scallions
3 TBSP	minced fresh ginger
½	red pepper, *diced*
¼ CUP	fresh cilantro
20	spring roll wrappers
•	oil, *for frying*

INSTRUCTIONS

1. In a medium bowl, combine duck meat with allspice, star anise, soy sauce, brown sugar, rice vinegar, and sesame oil. Marinate for 2 hours.

2. Preheat oven to 350°F. Place duck with marinade into a baking pan; bake, uncovered, for 20 minutes. Let cool.

3. Using two forks, shred the duck meat. Return to pan. Add daikon, scallions, ginger, red pepper, and cilantro. Mix well to coat in liquid. Drain off excess liquid.

4. Place 2 tablespoons filling in a 4-inch strip along the bottom-center of each spring roll wrapper. Fold in sides, then roll up tightly.

5. Heat 2 inches of oil in a frying pan over medium-high heat. Add spring rolls and fry until golden, 3-4 minutes. Serve with chili hoisin sauce, if desired.

Although star anise, anise (not related to star anise), and fennel seeds are different spices in the same botanical family, they all contain anethol, which gives them the similar licorice flavor. Star anise has little pods that form together into a star shape. Although it's not edible, it's commonly used in marinades, brines, or poaching liquids. Fennel, which has a milder licorice flavor, is more accessible to the home cook.

Want to dip? Serve these alongside a chili hoisin sauce: Combine 3 tablespoons soy sauce, 1 tablespoon sweet chili sauce, 1 tablespoon hoisin sauce, 2 tablespoons sesame oil, and 1 tablespoon honey.

Since all duck meat is essentially dark, home cooks can use either the breast or the dark meat for this recipe (rather than half and half). We made use of a whole duck by using the dark meat; we saved the breasts to prepare Duck with Sour Cherry Reduction (page 152). If your butcher only sells whole frozen duck, buy your duck ahead of time and ask your butcher to cut it into pieces for you once it defrosts.

SMOKED SHORT RIB TACOS

RESERVE CUT
A MODERN STEAKHOUSE

RESERVE CUT

OWNER/CHEF

*Owner Albert Allaham /
Chef Hok Chin*

LOCATION

*Downtown Manhattan,
New York*

NEW YORK CITY

Reserve Cut is kosher's most pampered experience. Located in Downtown Manhattan, the setting is one of the most glamorous in the city, kosher or non-kosher. From entry to exit, every aspect of your visit is five star, from the impeccable service to the classic and flawlessly executed menu.

The evening (or afternoon) begins as you enter via the glass-walled wine cellar. The sleek, spacious restaurant seats 200, and features a unique glass-walled open kitchen (that's where we like to sit). There are various party options, including use of the breathtaking private dining room housed within the wine cellar.

In the main dining room, there's plenty of room between tables to enjoy privacy as the wait staff stays attentive to your every need. The service has made Reserve Cut a go-to favorite for both business lunches and special-occasion dinners.

All the dishes, from appetizers to desserts, are magnificently presented. Start with the most popular appetizer, these Smoked Short Rib Tacos, or try Wagyu Angus Ribs or King Salmon Sashimi. Even the side dishes, like Mashed Potato with Black Truffles, are luxurious. End with Raspberry Crème Brûlée or Warm Almond Cake.

Reserve Cut is especially known for its superior cuts of meat; not only is the meat super prime; each cut is also butchered to perfection and trimmed of excess fat, making every bite perfect. The sommelier will help you pair that perfect steak with a selection from the extensive wine list. **- L.**

SMOKED SHORT RIB TACOS

YIELD
24 mini tacos

CATEGORY meat

DESCRIPTION

Hand-shredded prime beef in fried wonton wrappers

At Reserve Cut, this appetizer is served with a pineapple, tomato, and cilantro salsa. Add red onion, a finely diced jalapeño pepper, lime juice, salt, pepper, and olive oil.

INGREDIENTS

2 Tbsp	vegetable oil
5 lb	boneless lean beef short ribs, *cut into 3-inch pieces*
1 tsp	kosher salt
½ tsp	fresh ground black pepper
4	garlic cloves, *coarsely chopped*
1	*(16-oz)* can tomato sauce
1 cup	barbeque sauce
1 cup	beef stock
¼ cup	apple cider vinegar
½ tsp	ground mustard
3	smoked jalapeños *(also known as chipotle chilies)*
•	salt and pepper, *to taste*
24	fried wonton wrappers, *see note on facing page*

INSTRUCTIONS

1 Preheat oven to 325°F.

2 Heat oil over medium heat in a large, heavy, oven-safe pot or Dutch oven; brown the ribs on all sides, about 5 minutes, working in batches if necessary. Sprinkle ribs with salt and black pepper as they brown. Transfer cooked ribs to paper towels to absorb extra oil.

3 Stir garlic into remaining oil in pan; cook until fragrant, about 1 more minute. Mix in tomato sauce, barbeque sauce, beef stock, vinegar, mustard, and jalapeños. Bring sauce to a boil; lower heat and simmer for 1 minute to blend flavors. Stir in browned ribs.

4 Cover the pot and bake in the preheated oven until the rib meat is very tender, about 2½ hours. Turn the ribs occasionally while cooking.

5 Shred beef using two forks. Season with salt and pepper. Place into a clean pan; add some of the cooking sauce. Heat until warm. Fill fried wonton wrappers with shredded beef (see note on frying wontons).

CLOSER LOOK *A chipotle chili is a jalapeño pepper that has been smoked and dried ("chipotle" means "smoked"). The chilies require a hechsher. The chipotle imparts a smoky flavor to this dish. There are many different kinds of chilies, though, if you find a different type, you'll still get the kick without the smoke. Kosher chipotles are easily found online.*

To shred the beef more quickly, you might want to try a cooking tool called a "claw."

There are a few ways to fry wonton wrappers so they take the shape of a taco. To shape them perfectly, like the restaurant does, you'll need a taco shell deep fryer basket. A taco shell maker/taco press, which looks like tongs, will also shape a wonton as it fries, but you have to fry them one at a time. You can make a mini taco shell without any gadgets, though. Heat oil in a sauté pan or skillet. Fold the wonton wrapper in half and dip one side into the hot oil. Use a fork to press it down at the bottom. Use tongs to hold the top half in place. Once the bottom becomes stiff and crisp, flip and fry the opposite side.

"Allaham" means "butcher" in Arabic. The family of Albert Allaham, the owner of Reserve Cut (and cousin to Prime Hospitality Group owner Joey Allaham), had been butchers in Syria for over 200 years. Albert Allaham's family were among the final group of Jews to leave Syria in the 1990s, ending a century of migration to Brooklyn. In 2008, the family opened The Prime Cut in the heart of Syrian-Jewish Flatbush on Avenue U. The shop is renowned for its superior cuts of meat.

BEEF TINGA SLIDERS

LA GONDOLA RESTAURANT

LA GONDOLA

OWNER/CHEF
Owner/Chef Nir Weinblut

LOCATION
Beverly Hills, California

We had been waiting for a burger like this.

Open since 1992, La Gondola is Los Angeles's longest-standing kosher meat restaurant. ("That's like 100 years old in restaurant years," jokes owner Chef Nir Weinblut.)

Away from the Pico strip, La Gondola is located in the heart of Beverly Hills, near the area's upscale shops and hotels. (The restaurant also caters weddings and other events in the area's fine hotels.)

It's not ironic that the restaurant that's been around the longest is also completely innovative. This is where trends originate.

I got to know Chef Nir when I interviewed him recently about his experiences preparing gourmet kosher meals for a delegation of Jews traveling to the super lux city of Dubai, United Arab Emirates. A few of those meals broke world records for being the highest kosher meals ever served (at the top of the Burj Khalifa, the world's tallest building).

At La Gondola, all the food is flavorful and elegantly presented, but some dishes are legendary, such as the ribs, the Avocado Spring Rolls with Cilantro-Nut Dipping Sauce, the Shredded Asian Chicken appetizer — and these Beef Tinga Sliders. - V.

BEEF TINGA SLIDERS

YIELD

24 mini burgers (you will have extra tinga)

CATEGORY *meat*

DESCRIPTION

Mini lamb and beef sliders with shredded beef tinga

We love these little sliders topped with the pickles from Milt's BBQ (page 56). Where else but in this cookbook can you mix and match kosher restaurant recipes in one meal? For more menu ideas, see section divider pages.

For perfectly sized mini burgers and mini buns, each of your sliders should use about 1⅓ ounces of dough and buns about 1¼ ounces. each.

INGREDIENTS

BEEF TINGA:

3-4 LB	fatty brisket *(second cut is the best for this dish)*
1 TSP	kosher salt
1 TSP	freshly ground black pepper
1 TSP	onion powder
1 TBSP	finely chopped fresh garlic
1 TSP	fresh thyme
3 TBSP	oil
2	red onions, *in ½-inch slices*
2	carrots, *in ¼-inch slices*
3	celery ribs, *in ¼-inch slices*
2 CUPS	red wine
5 CUPS	veal stock, *divided*
3 TBSP	tomato paste

LAMB & BEEF SLIDERS:

1 LB	ground lamb
1 LB	ground beef
1 TBSP	chopped fresh parsley
1 TBSP	chopped fresh dill
4 TSP	chopped garlic
1 TSP	kosher salt
1 TSP	white pepper
1½ TSP	cumin
24	Mini Slider Buns
•	pickles, *optional*

INSTRUCTIONS

1 Prepare the Tinga: Preheat oven to 350°F. If the brisket is too large for your pan, cut meat into 2 even pieces. Rub brisket with salt, pepper, onion powder, garlic, and thyme.

2 Heat oil in a large skillet over medium heat. Add meat and sear on both sides.

3 Place vegetables into a large roasting pan. Place seared brisket over vegetables. Pour wine and 3 cups stock over meat. Cover and bake 3½-4 hours.

4 Remove brisket from roasting pan and place on a cutting board. Using two forks or your hands, pull brisket apart (it should be very tender).

5 Place liquid and vegetables from roasting pan into a food processor or blender and blend until smooth. In a medium bowl, whisk together tomato paste and remaining 2 cups veal stock. Add to food processor; blend.

6 Combine the sauce and pulled beef in a large skillet over medium-high heat. Bring to a boil. Reduce heat to low and simmer for 45 minutes (add roux if you would like to thicken the sauce further).

7 Prepare the sliders: In a medium bowl, combine lamb, beef, parsley, dill, garlic, salt, pepper, and cumin. Form into 24 equal-size patties, about ½-inch thick. Place patties onto a baking sheet and refrigerate for 1 hour.

8 Grease and heat a grill or grill pan. Add patties and cook until medium rare, about 3 minutes per side.

9 To serve, place each slider into a bun. Top with pulled brisket and pickles.

MINI SLIDER BUNS

1 CUP	warm water
¼ CUP	sugar
1 TBSP	instant yeast
2 TBSP	margarine
1 LARGE	egg
3½ CUPS	unbleached all-purpose flour
1¼ TSP	kosher salt
1 TBSP	margarine, *melted*
1 TBSP	poppy or sesame seeds

1 In the bowl of an electric mixer fitted with a dough hook, combine water, sugar, and yeast. Mix to combine. Add margarine, egg, flour, and salt. Knead until dough is soft and smooth and does not stick to the sides of the bowl. Remove dough from mixer. Place into a large bowl. Cover and let rise 1-2 hours, until doubled in size (this will happen faster in a warm area of the kitchen).

2 Lightly grease a baking sheet or line with parchment paper. Gently deflate the dough and divide into 24 even-sized pieces. Shape each piece into a ball. Place balls onto prepared baking sheet. Flatten, using the palm of your hand or a second baking sheet. Allow to rise, 45-60 minutes. Buns will puff up again.

3 Preheat oven to 375°F. Brush buns with melted margarine and sprinkle with poppy or sesame seeds. Bake for 12-16 minutes, until golden. Let cool.

4 To serve, slice cooled buns and enjoy with sliders and pulled beef.

HUEVOS MOTULEÑOS

MEXIKOSHER

OWNER/CHEF
Owner/Chef Katsuji Tanabe

LOCATION
*Los Angeles,
California*

Mexikosher is definitely a stop for the adventurous foodie who wants a little bit of the cultural diversity that Chef Kat brings to a dish.

Culinary prodigy Katsube Tanabe grew up in Mexico, to a Japanese father and Mexican mother. He came to L.A. at age 19, working his way up in upscale restaurants and attending Le Cordon Bleu. Then Shiloh's recognized his emerging talent and tapped him to become their next chef. Chef Kat loved the challenge of kosher food, and cooked there for six years before opening Mexikosher.

Huevos Motuleños, one of the dishes that appear on Chef Kat's blackboards, is a traditional breakfast in the Yucatan region of Mexico … even if the ingredients don't seem to relate to breakfast.

Some famous dishes at Mexikosher? There's birria, a lamb-and-beef chili that's braised for 16 hours and served over nachos … or the carnitas, the 19-hour braised beef-and-duck confit. Here's a quicker taste of what Mexikosher is about. **-L.**

HUEVOS MOTULEÑOS

YIELD *2 servings*

CATEGORY *meat*

DESCRIPTION

Fried eggs and refried beans over a fried tortilla, served with salsa, turkey, and plantains

We topped our Huevos Motuleños with sunnyside-up eggs, but to prepare your eggs over easy, as Chef Kat recommends, carefully flip the eggs to cook on both sides, leaving the yolk intact.

INGREDIENTS

REFRIED BEANS:

4 TSP	olive oil
1 SMALL	onion, *chopped*
1	garlic clove, *crushed*
2 CUPS	cooked black beans
½ TSP	kosher salt
1	bunch fresh epazote, *chopped*

SALSA:

4	tomatoes
1 SMALL	onion
1	habanero pepper
•	kosher salt

PLANTAIN:

2 TBSP	oil
1	ripe plantain, *peeled and sliced*

FOR ASSEMBLY:

•	oil, *for frying*
2	tortillas
2	eggs over easy
¼ CUP	cooked peas
4 OZ	smoked turkey breast, *chopped*
2 TBSP	nondairy sour cream *(optional)*

INSTRUCTIONS

1 Prepare the refried beans: Heat oil in a sauté pan over medium heat. Add onion and garlic and sauté until onions are soft, 7 minutes. Add beans and cook an additional 8-10 minutes. Using a potato masher or a fork, mash beans until they have a smooth texture. Season with salt. Remove from heat and stir in epazote.

2 Prepare the salsa: Preheat oven to broil. Place the tomatoes, onion, and habanero pepper into a baking pan. Broil until charred, about 10 minutes. Transfer to a blender or food processor and blend. Season with salt to taste.

3 Prepare the plantain: Heat oil in a sauté pan over medium heat. Add plaintain and sauté until golden brown, about 10 minutes. Set aside.

4 To assemble, heat oil in a frying pan over medium heat. Add tortillas, one at a time, and fry for a few seconds (they should remain soft and and not get crispy). Place each tortilla on a plate. Spread with refried beans and top with an egg and salsa. Sprinkle with peas and turkey. Top with nondairy sour cream (optional). Serve the plantain on the side.

In 2013, Chef Kat won the title "Chopped Champion." His entrée dish was lamb shawarma with mole sauce, which included dried chilies, tomatoes, and onions. He's also a competitive hockey player.

Epazote is a strong-flavored herb used in Mexican cuisine and the secret ingredient to great refried beans and other Mexican dishes. It should be available at your local Mexican market.

"My cooking is all about honoring family and tradition, with recipes passed from generation to generation. My chef training helps me to offer new interpretations, especially as a kosher chef, but the joy of cooking will always rely upon the joy given to those that I am serving, whether they be my family or my customers. Cooking becomes personal only when it is offered from the heart."

- CHEF KATSUJI TANABE, MEXIKOSHER

BASIL FRIES

BASIL
PIZZA & WINE BAR ®

BASIL PIZZA AND WINE BAR

OWNER/CHEF

Owner Dani Branover / Chef José E. Soto

LOCATION

The Crown Heights neighborhood of Brooklyn, New York

When it opened, Basil made news by breaking the mold of kosher restaurants. Here was a hip place that you could experience something a little different, where the menu was seasonal, exciting, and tapped the diversity of New York. Why stick to salmon and tilapia when you're so close to the greatest fish market in the world? (Basil's menu lives up to that vision and incorporates inventive uses of kosher's full selection of fish in dishes such as Smoked Bluefish, Arctic Char Crudo, and Hake Fillet with a Beurre Blanc Sauce.)

When owner Dani Bronover first moved to Crown Heights from Israel, he searched the neighborhood for a good cup of coffee and a croissant — and couldn't find it. He went beyond that vision when opening Basil, in a location that was off the beaten path from the Jewish neighborhood and attracts a diverse clientele, who sit at small tables, perch on stools at tall family-style tables, or dine al fresco.

Today, Chef José E. Soto keeps the menu updated seasonally. Regulars can look forward to trying new, exciting dishes or coming back for their favorites, like the Wild Mushroom Pizza with goat cheese and truffle oil, Sweet Yam Gnocchi with homemade mascarpone cheese, or these signature Basil Fries. Since Basil's inception, these quickly became a dish that people traveled to try (and most of Basil's hundreds of visitors a day do come from outside the neighborhood). -**L**.

BASIL FRIES

YIELD *2-4 servings*

CATEGORY *dairy*

DESCRIPTION

Fries with garlic-truffle mayo and Parmesan

When we asked various chefs for French fry tips, they all told us that the best potato to use is the pricey Kennebec. It's rare to find the Kennebec in grocery stores. Finer restaurants buy these potatoes through suppliers.

INGREDIENTS

5	Idaho potatoes, *sliced into French fries*
•	oil, *for frying*
2	pinches kosher salt
•	pinch freshly ground black pepper or crushed peppercorns
•	pinch chopped fresh parsley
1 Tbsp	freshly grated Parmesan cheese

TRUFFLE MAYONNAISE:

4	egg yolks
1	whole egg
1 tsp	fresh lemon juice
1 tsp	white wine vinegar
1½ cups	canola oil
2 tsp	kosher salt
¼ cup	extra virgin olive oil
½ cup	truffle oil
1 Tbsp	roasted garlic

INSTRUCTIONS

1 Rinse cut potatoes well with cold water to remove the starch (this prevents them from sticking together). Drain and dry completely to avoid splattering.

2 Prepare the mayonnaise: In a blender or food processor (a Vitamix is recommended), combine egg yolks, egg, lemon juice, and vinegar. Blend for 30 seconds. Add canola oil in a slow stream while blending; blend until emulsified. Add salt. Continue to blend while adding olive oil in a slow stream. Finally, slowly add in truffle oil while blending. Add roasted garlic.

3 Heat oil in a deep fryer to 250°F. Add French fries and fry for 5-6 minutes. Remove from oil and place on a baking sheet. Place sheet in the refrigerator for ½ hour, until French fries are cold.

4 Heat oil in a deep fryer to 350°F. Add cooled French fries and fry again for 2-3 minutes, until golden and crisp. Season with salt, pepper, and parsley. Sprinkle with Parmesan cheese.

5 Serve truffle mayonnaise in a ramekin alongside fries.

The truffle mayo will yield about 3 cups, more than you need for the fries. Use it for all your mayo and dipping needs all week, or divide recipe in half (the only challenge will be splitting the whole egg).

Chef Soto recommends D'Allesandro Truffle Oil, the brand used in the restaurant.

He's incredibly innovative with dairy cuisine; that's why it's very ironic that Chef Soto's favorite food is steak.

"Home cooks have an advantage. They don't need to get caught up with trendy ingredients and trendy food. Just cook good, comforting food that tastes good. There's no need to outdo yourself."

- OWNER DANIEL BRANOVER

POPOVER POTATOES

CHAGALL BISTRO

OWNER/CHEF
Owners Dan & Sonia Halimi / Executive Chef Jean Claude Teulade

---

LOCATION

The Park Slope neighborhood of Brooklyn, New York

Chagall is a very classical — and classy — authentic French bistro.

Chef Jean Claude Teulade is not afraid to experiment with interesting ingredients (such as various types of offal), which make the Chagall experience unique; it's intimate enough for dinner for two, but large enough to celebrate a special occasion with a larger group.

The beginnings of Chagall are as charming as the atmosphere. Paris-born owners Dan and Sonia Halimi were in the United States, contemplating moving to this country. While walking in Park Slope, they saw a nonkosher French bistro for sale. This would be their piece of France in America. They purchased the restaurant, left their jobs and home in Paris, and turned the nonkosher Belleville into the kosher Chagall.

Everything at Chagall has flavor — that's largely the result of starting most of the dishes with their house-made stocks. To begin the meal, standouts include the "Foie Gras" Brulée, the Warm Beef Tongue with Tarragon Sabayon Sauce, Steak Tartare, and Caramelized Onion Tart topped with Frisée Salad.

Every dish sounds very complicated. So what are home cooks to do when trying to determine which Chagall dish we'd bring into our home kitchens?

That's when owner Sonia suggested this addictive side, which features the creaminess of mashed potatoes and the crispiness of a fry, in pretty little meringue-like mounds. Still very French in technique, but this one was simple. - **V.**

POPOVER POTATOES

YIELD *4-6 servings*

CATEGORY *pareve*

DESCRIPTION

Mounds of mashed potatoes with a crispy exterior and creamy interior

Just like the food, all of the furnishings at Chagall are authentically French, having been imported from France by the previous owners after gracing old brasseries in Paris.

INGREDIENTS

2 LB	*(about 4)* Russet Idaho potatoes
2 CUPS	cold water
1 TSP	kosher salt
2 STICKS	unsalted margarine, *cut into bits*
•	pinch freshly grated nutmeg
½ LB	flour *(see note)*
8	eggs
•	oil, *for frying*

INSTRUCTIONS

1 Preheat oven to 425°F. Bake potatoes until soft, 1 hour. Let cool.

2 Scoop out the potato flesh and pass through a food mill. You should have about 2 cups.

3 In a medium saucepan, combine cold water, salt, margarine, and nutmeg. Bring to a boil. Add flour and, using a wooden spoon, stir vigorously until dough pulls away from the sides of the pan.

4 Transfer dough to the bowl of an electric mixer. With the mixer running on low, add eggs, one at a time, beating after each addition. Add potato and mix well to combine.

5 Using a flat-bottomed sauté pan, heat 1½ inches oil to 350°F. Transfer potato mixture to a large pastry bag. Pipe directly into the oil (the bottom of the potato puffs will rest at the bottom of the pan, with just the tips exposed to air. If you have too much oil, the potato puffs will float and not form their meringue shape). Fry in batches until golden and crisp, about 3 minutes. Transfer to a paper-towel-lined plate to drain.

We tried many times, but couldn't duplicate Chagall's mound-shaped popover potatoes when piping directly into a deep-fryer, as they do in the restaurant. For us home cooks, frying in a sauté pan, though, worked perfectly.

½ pound flour is about 1½ cups, but if you have a digital scale, use it.

Don't have a food mill? Mash your potatoes very well with a masher.

Popover potatoes are my favorite as a teaser, paired with a chilled Loire Valley White Wine (with flavors of peach) or a Grapefruit and Rose de Provence cocktail for aperitif. Bon appétit! Gastronomically yours,

-EXECUTIVE CHEF
JC TEULADE,
CHAGALL BISTRO

SWEET PICKLES

MILT'S

BARBECUE FOR THE PERPLEXED

MILT'S BARBECUE FOR THE PERPLEXED

OWNER/CHEF

Chef Bryan Gryka

LOCATION

The Lakeview neighborhood of Chicago, Illinois

ILLINOIS

I first learned about Milt's when my husband traveled there on business and called me up, crying that he'd just eaten the best burger of his life: The Milt's Burger. Since then, he calls Milt's "a place worth flying to Chicago to eat at."

He took the chef's card, took a photo, and sent it to me immediately.

Chef Bryan Gryka has a lot of culinary tricks up his sleeve, and that burger isn't a simple feat. I learned that it's topped with brisket, chili, "bacon," crispy onions, and bbq aioli … oh, and there's a house-made bun (seven recipes for one burger!)

Lots of the items on Milt's barbecue-central menu are smoked, like the popular spare ribs or the Smoked Brisket Chili. So what part of the Milt's repertoire is possible for us to bring into our kitchens that aren't equipped with smokers?

One of the items that we kept hearing visitors to Milt's mention were the bread-and-butter pickles that are placed on the table to start the meal … and how they'd keep on requesting more and more pickles. Pickles? That sounds like something we could do. Chef Bryan, could you tell us how you make your pickles? - V.

SWEET PICKLES

YIELD *1 quart*

CATEGORY *pareve*

DESCRIPTION

Sweet and spicy house-made pickles, served on every table to start the meal

Pickling salt is finer than kosher salt and dissolves easily in brine. Unlike table salt, it doesn't contain any iodine or anti-caking ingredients that affect the pickles. If you don't have pickling salt, Diamond kosher salt is the best alternative.

INGREDIENTS

1	yellow onion, *puréed in a food processor*
1 CUP	white vinegar
2 CUPS	apple cider vinegar
2 CUPS	plus 2 Tbsp sugar
2 TBSP	mustard seed
1 TSP	celery seed
½ TSP	turmeric
¾ TSP	red pepper flakes
2 TBSP	Ball's or Morton's pickling salt
1 TSP	pickling spice
3	English cucumbers, *sliced*
1	yellow onion, *sliced*

INSTRUCTIONS

1 In a large saucepan, combine puréed onion, vinegars, sugar, mustard seed, celery seed, turmeric, red pepper flakes, pickling salt, and pickling spice. Bring to a simmer.

2 Place cucumbers and sliced onion into a stainless steel bowl. Pour the hot liquid over the vegetables until they are fully submerged. Place a non-reactive bowl over the vegetables to help keep them submerged in the liquid. Let cool.

3 Once cool, transfer pickles with juice to an airtight container and refrigerate. Will be ready the next day, but taste best after 2 weeks. Keep refrigerated for up to 3 months.

CHEF BRYAN ON "WHAT MAKES A GREAT DISH"

- *Don't be afraid of simplicity. One of the biggest mistakes cooks can make is to over-think their food.*

- *One of the most important aspects of quality food is balancing different flavors. A good ratio of heat, sweet, salt, sour, bitter, and umami will transform your dish from good to extraordinary.*

- *The key to good BBQ is low and slow. You can't rush good food.*

- *Being timid with your food shows in the final product. Don't be afraid to think outside the box.*

POUTINE

PizzaPita
Pasta Bar - Restaurant - Bar à Pâtes

PIZZA PITA

OWNER/CHEF
Owner Chaim Shpigelman

LOCATION
Montreal, Canada

CANADA

Poutine is a very sensitive subject when you talk to Montreal Canadians. They all have their own vision of what the perfect poutine tastes like. Luckily, they all agreed that Pizza Pita's version is perfect.

Poutine and Pizza Pita are an integral part of their memories. They tell us, "I think of Motza'ei Shabbos, friends, snow, and good times together eating cheesy, runny fries" … "We'd always get together there after school … it's a pizza store that hasn't been replicated. New York-style pizza doesn't offer what they offer."

What does that mean? New York has lots of pizza shops.

"It's the friendly, small-town feel. The owner always says *hi* as if he remembers us, even if we were small when we used to come often, and now we're grown and we visit the pizza shop when we go back to Montreal for a visit."

Owner Chaim Shpigelman was as obliging to us as he is to his customers and took up the challenge to recreate this dish using ingredients that are available to the consumer. We were very skeptical when we saw the list of ingredients. This is what's in poutine that our Montreal friends dream about?

It wasn't until we put them together and tasted that we understood. -L.

POUTINE

YIELD *2 large servings*

CATAGORY *dairy*

DESCRIPTION

French fries topped with a gravy-like sauce and cheese

You can make poutine using baked French fries, frozen French fries, or the fries from your own local pizza shop. You can also try it with either spicy or sweet fries.

This might be a service that's exclusive to out-of-town pizza shops, but at Pizza Pita, they'll happily customize their dishes and prepare what you want, even if it's not on the menu.

INGREDIENTS

2 CUPS	cold water
1	*(2-oz)* pouch "Serve-a-Gravy" or pareve gravy mix
2 TSP	pareve consommé powder
1 LB	potatoes, *cut into French fries*
	oil, *for frying*
5 OZ	mozzarella cheese, *grated*

INSTRUCTIONS

1 In a small saucepan, combine water, gravy mix, and consommé powder. Bring to a boil. Reduce heat to medium; cook until thickened.

2 Meanwhile, heat oil to 365°F. Add French fries and fry until light golden brown, about 5 minutes. Remove French fries from oil and divide between 2 deep dishes. Sprinkle immediately with cheese and top with gravy. Allow 1-2 minutes for cheese to melt and serve.

Poutine, traditionally made with fresh cheese curds and gravy, was invented in rural Quebec in the 1950s. Lots of towns claim to be its birthplace. The popularity of the dish later spread throughout Quebec and Canada.

YAKISOBA PAN NOODLES

Sushi Metsuyan is your neighborhood Pan-Asian restaurant (and since there are three locations, that's a lot of neighborhoods) with fantastic staples that regulars order again and again, but definitely too many yummy dishes for just one visit. Get a soup to start the meal (like the Udon Soup), a fun appetizer (like the Avocado Eggroll with Plum Dipping Sauce), exotic salads, and enjoy massive portions for the main courses, like the favorite, tender "Metsuyan" Korean Ribs, or Chilean Sea Bass Dumplings wrapped in napa cabbage. Sushi lovers will also be in their element, starting a meal with a Bonzai Kani Salad and enjoying rolls like the 5 Alarm, Volcano, Godzilla, and much more.

And though it offers sophisticated dishes, there are lots of choices for the kids too in the family-friendly restaurant. The kids will also be entertained by the entrancing fish tank which runs the length of an entire wall in all Sushi Metsuyan locations. -L.

SUSHI METSUYAN

LOCATION
Cedarhurst, NY; Teaneck, NJ; Kew Garden Hills in Queens, NY

YAKISOBA PAN NOODLES

YIELD *6-8 servings*

CATEGORY
pareve or meat

DESCRIPTION
Wok-seared noodles with aromatics, spices, and a medley of vegetables

You can also make this recipe using frozen lo mein noodles prepared according to package instructions.

INGREDIENTS

1 LB	whole wheat thin spaghetti, *prepared according to package instructions*
½ TSP	kosher salt
⅛ TSP	freshly ground black pepper
•	pinch curry powder
¼ TSP	cayenne pepper
•	few Tbsp oil
1	onion, *cut into thin strips*
2	Portobello mushroom caps, *sliced, gills removed*
1 CUP	carrots, *julienned*
1 CUP	shredded cabbage
1 TBSP	chopped fresh cilantro
½ CUP	chicken stock
•	splash sweet teriyaki sauce
•	chopped scallions

INSTRUCTIONS

1 Season the pasta with salt, pepper, curry powder, and cayenne pepper. Set aside.

2 Heat oil in a wok or sauté pan over medium heat. Add onion; sauté until soft, 7 minutes. Add mushrooms and carrot; sauté 3-4 minutes. Add cabbage and cilantro; cook 2-3 minutes. Add noodles; stir to combine. Add chicken stock to coat pasta. Drizzle with sweet teriyaki sauce; garnish with scallions.

EGGPLANT GHETTO STYLE

GAM GAM KOSHER RESTAURANT

OWNER/CHEF
Owners Ramy & Shachar Banin

LOCATION
Jewish Ghetto, Venice, Italy

In Venice, just outside the world's oldest Jewish ghetto, overlooking Canal Canareggio, is Italy's kosher oasis. Gam Gam, part of the Venetian streetscape for 15 years, allows kosher travelers to savor the Italian experience of dining alongside a canal as gondolas and water taxis glide by.

The portions at Gam Gam are generous and the menu choices are diverse, encompassing both authentic Jewish and Italian foods. Begin with the Israeli Appetizers with Falafels, a tapas-style appetizer dish, where you'll be served nine small plates of different dips and vegetables, including chickpeas four ways, hot pepper sauce, eggplant dip, egg salad, tomato salad, marinated sweet peppers, and more. And though all the Middle Eastern-style dishes are the best anywhere, Gam Gam still stays true to its location, with authentic Italian pasta dishes (such as the Pappardelle with Mushrooms) and many traditional Venetian dishes, like this eggplant, which is part of the culinary legacy of Venetian Jews (the family of one Venetian Jew on the restaurant's staff traces his family's history in Venice back to the 15th century).

The restaurant is run by Chabad *shluchim* Rabbi Ramy and Shachar Banin, and helps fund their efforts to bring Jews back to their heritage and life back to the ghetto. The Shabbat hospitality at Gam Gam is renowned—with Jews coming together from all over the world, the atmosphere is warm and welcoming, and the food is fresh and refreshing.

If you'll be continuing your travels after dining at Gam Gam, you can take along some baked goods and fresh authentic Italian pizza, available at the sister bakery, Gam Gam Goodies. -L.

EGGPLANT GHETTO STYLE

YIELD *2-4 servings*

CATEGORY *pareve*

DESCRIPTION

Crispy eggplant strips sautéed in garlic-infused oil

Gam in Hebrew means "also," as in Jewish and also Italian food.

INGREDIENTS

6	garlic cloves, *crushed*
¼ CUP	olive oil
1	eggplant
3 TBSP	oil
½ TSP	kosher salt
•	pinch coarse black pepper
1 TBSP	finely chopped fresh parsley

INSTRUCTIONS

1 Prepare the olive oil-garlic infusion: In a small bowl, combine garlic and olive oil. Cover and refrigerate overnight.

2 Using a sharp knife and cutting lengthwise, remove the skin of the eggplant, including some of the flesh. You should have long, vertical strips. Reserve the interior flesh of the eggplant for another use.

3 Lay the eggplant slices on your work surface, flesh side down; cut eggplant into ¼-in strips on an angle.

4 Heat oil in a large saute pan. Add eggplant strips and season with salt and pepper. Add olive oil-garlic infusion and saute until eggplant is thoroughly cooked and some of the skins are crispy. Garnish with fresh parsley.

WANT MORE SIDES?

Here's where you'll find more side dishes throughout this book.

FAMILY NIGHTS

A COZY WINTER NIGHT

Sweet Potato Soup
(page 72)

AND

Popcorn Chicken
(page 132)

OR

Bolognese
(page 182)

KID-FRIENDLY DINNER NIGHT

Chicken Fingers
+ Cranberry BBQ
Dipping Sauce
(page 128)

AND

Beer-Battered
Onion Rings
(page 167)

OR

The Cedarhurst
Sandwich
(page 136)

LIGHT NIGHT

Blackened Fish
(page 202)

OR

Salmon with
Lemon & Caper
Sauce
(page 206)

AND

Darna's Salad
(page 84)

FUN NIGHT!

Taco Supreme Salad
(page 110)

Pizza de Nonna
(page 233)

Poutine
(page 60)

PIZAZA
Milkshakes
(page 244)

Cereal Milk
Ice Cream
(page 276)

SOUPS & SALADS

"WORRIES GO DOWN BETTER WITH SOUP."
~*Jewish Proverb*

SWEET POTATO SOUP

CITRON + ROSE

CITRON & ROSE

OWNER/CHEF
Chef Karen Nicolas

LOCATION
Philadelphia, Pennsylvania

PENNSYLVANIA

Lots of our friends forgo a trip to Manhattan in favor of Philadelphia when they want to visit their "absolutely favorite" restaurant. And if you're already in New York, it's still worth the drive. For a family-friendly experience, try their sister restaurant, C & R Kitchen, in the Merion Station neighborhood of Philadelphia.

Citron & Rose feels like a place where you want to spend time. The decor is modern, upbeat, and inviting. The seasonal food comes out gorgeously plated.

The most fascinating part about Citron & Rose's cuisine is the perspective.

Chef Karen Nicolas wasn't familiar with Jewish food before she arrived at Citron & Rose, but she makes it exciting to see the traditional ingredients — from both European and Middle Eastern Jewish dishes — used to create cuisine that is completely modern and refined, but still familiar.

It's a fine dining experience that embraces our culture at the same time. - V.

SWEET POTATO SOUP

YIELD *4 servings*

CATEGORY *meat*

DESCRIPTION

Sweet potato soup with beef chorizo meatballs, cucumbers, pea leaves, & red pepper paste

At Citron & Rose, the meatballs are plated in the soup in a dramatic straight line. We used a skewer to help achieve a similar look.

Optional garnishes:
- *sliced cucumbers*
- *pea leaves*
- *red pepper paste*

INGREDIENTS

SOUP:

2 TBSP	margarine
1 CUP	chopped onion
½ CUP	chopped fennel
½ CUP	chopped apple
¼ CUP	chopped celery
1½ LB	yams, *peeled, cut into 1-in pieces (about 5 cups)*
4 CUPS	water
1	*(8-oz)* can coconut milk
1	cinnamon stick
¼ TSP	ground nutmeg
2 TBSP	honey
2 TBSP	kosher salt

MEATBALLS:

¾-1 LB	ground beef *(80/20)*
2 TBSP	smoked paprika
2 TSP	dark chili powder
1 TSP	garlic powder
1 TSP	kosher salt
1 TSP	dried oregano
½ TSP	ground coriander
½ TSP	ground cumin
1½ TBSP	red wine vinegar
1	whole egg
⅓ CUP	dried breadcrumbs
1½ TBSP	soy milk

INSTRUCTIONS

1. Prepare the soup: Melt margarine in a large saucepan over medium heat. Add onion, fennel, apple, and celery; sweat vegetables until tender, about 10 minutes. Add yams, water, coconut milk, cinnamon stick, nutmeg, honey, and salt. Let simmer until sweet potatoes are tender, about 20 minutes. Discard the cinnamon stick. Purée soup in a blender until smooth.

2. Prepare the meatballs: Preheat oven to 350°F. Line or grease a baking sheet. In a large bowl, combine meat, spices, red wine vinegar, egg, breadcrumbs, and soy milk. Mix well. Shape into meatballs. Place on prepared baking sheet. Bake for 12-15 minutes, or until cooked through.

3. To serve, ladle soup into a wide, shallow bowl. Line up meatballs on one side. Garnish with cucumbers, pea leaves, and red pepper paste (optional).

DRESS UP YOUR SALAD

"I would say that home cooks should consider making their own dressing/vinaigrettes for their salads instead of buying them at a store. It's just a matter of a few simple and inexpensive ingredients, a bowl, and a whisk! Homemade dressing has a long storage life and will taste fresher and brighter than store-bought dressings, which have too many additives, thickeners, and preservatives that do not complement a healthy eating lifestyle. Below is a brown mustard vinaigrette we use in the restaurant. It goes great with fish and vegetables but also as a marinade for meats."

— CHEF KAREN NICOLAS, CITRON & ROSE

BROWN MUSTARD VINAIGRETTE

½ CUP	spicy brown mustard
½ CUP	white wine or champagne vinegar
1 CUP	vegetable oil
½ CUP	extra virgin olive oil
¼ CUP	water
½ CUP	minced shallots or red onion
3 LARGE	garlic cloves, *minced*
•	kosher salt and black pepper, *to taste*

○ Blend mustard, vinegar, oils, and water until smooth. Add in shallots and garlic; season with salt and pepper to taste.

FOOD & WINE *Food & Wine Magazine recognized Chef Karen Nicolas as one of "2012's Best New Chefs."*

PORTOBELLO MUSHROOM SOUP

OMNI
JEWELS & JAVA CAFE

JAVA CAFÉ

LOCATION
Toronto, Canada

CANADA

Some great restaurants happen by accident. It's always a good idea for businesses selling luxury products to pamper their customers. So, 15 years ago, the people at Omni Jewel Crafters thought it would be a great idea to serve their customers some coffee and homemade muffins …. I suppose the food was very popular, because the menu kept expanding until Java became the popular dairy restaurant and caterer that it is today.

Buy a lovely piece of jewelry and then celebrate the occasion with an elegant meal, ending off with a slice of Caramel Praline Cheesecake — sounds like a perfect day.

This is Java's iconic soup that's been on the menu for the past 12 years. - L.

PORTOBELLO MUSHROOM SOUP

YIELD *8 servings*

CATEGORY *pareve*

DESCRIPTION

Sautéed Portobello mushrooms cooked in a homemade vegetable stock and blended until smooth

The salt content of commercial vegetable stocks and your own homemade stock will vary. No matter which you're using, taste after blending to determine the right amount of additional salt needed, if any.

INGREDIENTS

2 Tbsp   oil

1 LARGE   sweet onion, *diced*

2   garlic cloves, *minced*

2 LB   *(about 8 large)* Portobello mushrooms, *gills removed, finely diced*

10 CUPS   homemade vegetable stock *(recipe follows), divided*

• kosher salt, *to taste (see note)*

• pinch coarse black pepper

INSTRUCTIONS

1 Heat oil in a large stockpot over medium heat. Add onion and garlic and sauté until onion is soft, about 7 minutes.

2 Lower heat, add mushrooms, and cook very slowly, until most of the mushroom liquid has evaporated, 20-25 minutes. (Patience when eliminating the water in the mushrooms in this step will make the difference between a rich and flavorful soup and a watery soup.)

3 Add 2 cups stock and simmer until thickened, about 5 minutes. Add remaining vegetable stock and bring to a boil. Cook for 45-60 minutes.

4 Purée in a blender until smooth. Season with salt and pepper.

HOMEMADE VEGETABLE STOCK

At Java, this broth is a must-have base for soups, sauces, and many other dishes.

- a variety of vegetables *(onions, carrots, celery, zucchini, cabbage, and/ or green beans)*
- your choice of seasoning *(kosher salt, pepper, garlic, and bay leaves)*
- water

1 Place vegetables and seasonings into a large pot. Cover with water and bring to a boil.

2 Reduce heat and let simmer for 1 hour. Strain. Your broth is now ready to use.

CLOSER LOOK *Cremini and baby Bella mushrooms are simply younger (and hence, smaller) versions of Portobello (creminis are the smallest; baby Bellas are a week more mature). Because full-sized Portobellos ripen further, their gills darken. To save time, you can use pre-washed and sliced baby bella mushrooms in this recipe instead of Portobellos. You will still need to dice them finely. All sizes of the mushroom have a flavor that's much more intense than their white button cousins.*

CAULIFLOWER BISQUE

AMSTERDAM ★ BURGER ★ Co.

AMSTERDAM BURGER CO.

OWNER/CHEF
Owner/Chef Mike Gershkovich

LOCATION
Manhattan, Upper West Side, New York

NEW YORK CITY

Every time I have a conversation with Chef Mike Gershkovich, I feel like he's throwing an avalanche of culinary wisdom at me. I always rush to grab a pen and paper so I can take notes. I was writing very feverishly as he was telling me the techniques behind his super-velvety Cauliflower Bisque, Amsterdam Burger's signature soup.

In contrast to Chef Mike's fine-dining restaurant, Mike's Bistro (see page 152), Amsterdam Burger is a hip Upper West Side burger joint. It has a cool vibe, a casual atmosphere (the menu is on the placemats), and is a fun place to eat.

What's the perfect meal at Amsterdam Burger? Start with this signature soup, Yam Fritters with hot sauce, or Zucchini Fries with ranch sauce. (The sauces at Amsterdam Burger are really something special.) Regulars rave about the Breakfast Burger. Sip a Mint Lemonade, and finish your meal with the Peanut Butter Mousse, served in a Mason jar. - V.

CAULIFLOWER BISQUE

YIELD *4-6 servings*

CATEGORY *pareve*

DESCRIPTION

Smooth and thick cauliflower and parsnip soup topped with garlic crumbs (see note)

At Amsterdam Burger, the mashgiach (kashruth supervisor) thoroughly checks the fresh cauliflower, but what's a home cook to do when there's only frozen available? You can shred frozen cauliflower in your food processor. It needs to be firm to shred, so thaw only slightly.

INGREDIENTS

2	heads *(about 2½ pounds)* cauliflower, *shredded*
1	parsnip, *shredded*
½ TO ⅔ CUP	olive oil
1 TSP	kosher salt, *plus more to taste*
•	pinch coarse black pepper
¼ TSP	fresh thyme
1	bay leaf
4	garlic cloves, *thinly sliced*
•	water as needed

INSTRUCTIONS

1. In a large, heavy-bottomed saucepan over medium-low heat, combine cauliflower, parsnip, olive oil, salt, pepper, thyme, bay leaf, and garlic. Cover; let simmer for 20-40 minutes, until mixture is mushy. The salt will extract the natural moisture in the vegetables. Stir occasionally.

2. Add water to thin soup to the desired consistency. Let simmer for 10 minutes. Taste; adjust salt and pepper, if necessary. Transfer soup to a blender (or use an immersion blender); pureé until smooth.

At Amsterdam Burger, the Cauliflower Bisque is served with garlic crumbs. Cook peeled, whole garlic cloves in olive oil over low heat for about 10 minutes. Allow to cool for 30-45 minutes before using. Store at room temperature. Toss panko crumbs with the garlic-infused oil and toast in a 250ºF oven until crisp. Chef Mike also recommends serving this soup with a crostini rubbed with fresh garlic (as shown).

Do you usually start your soups by sautéing an onion? Chef Mike says it's the onion that keeps soup from attaining that truly buttery texture. That's because onions contain sugar, and sugar is a stabilizer that keeps the veggies from breaking apart. For velvety creaminess, sweat your vegetables without an onion or water.

DARNA'S SALAD

DARNA

OWNER/CHEF
Owner/Chef Ayelet Vahnish /
Owner Esther Dahan

LOCATION
Panama City, Panama

Panama City may seem distant and exotic, but it hosts a vibrant, blossoming Jewish community, buoyed by the commercial opportunities in the Panama Canal's business district.

Darna is the queen of Panama City's kosher restaurant scene, winning favor of both tourists and the locals, mostly Sephardic Jews.

Established in 2003 by sisters Esther Dahan and Ayelet Vahnish, the restaurant has grown to five locations, servicing all of kosher Panama City's culinary needs.

The original café, on Punta Pacifica in the Gran Plaza area, features a fusion of dishes, including fish dishes such as the Mediterranean Branzino and Moroccan Sea Bass, or this Darna Salad that can be seen on most tables.

Next door to the café is Darna's Boutique Gourmet, where customers can buy homemade breads and pastries (made fresh daily), as well as sauces, marmalades, spices, and a box of Darna's famous brownies.

Also in the Darna family is the meat restaurant, Lula by Darna, which features Moroccan-inspired cuisine.

The ambiance at each Darna location is charming and cozy; lots of attention has been paid to the details. It's just the spot to spend a lazy morning, nibbling on freshly baked bread while sipping coffee made with Darna's freshly roasted coffee beans (which come from the mountains of Panama), while perusing one of the books in the lending library. Idyllic? Yes. -L.

DARNA'S SALAD

YIELD *6 servings*

CATEGORY *dairy*

DESCRIPTION

Romaine salad with feta cheese and a sweet balsamic vinaigrette

"Darna" in Moroccan means "my house." That's the concept of the restaurants. The sisters want everyone to feel like a welcome part of the family as they enjoy good food and homemade pasta and bread.

INGREDIENTS

2 HEADS	Romaine lettuce, *chopped*
2	red peppers
2 MEDIUM	tomatoes, *cubed*
2	cucumbers, *cubed*
6-8	white button mushrooms, *sliced*
2 CUPS	grated or cubed feta cheese

DRESSING:

½ CUP	olive oil
¼ CUP	balsamic vinegar
1 TBSP	honey
1 TSP	Dijon mustard
•	kosher salt, *to taste*
•	coarse black pepper, *to taste*

INSTRUCTIONS

1. Preheat oven to 425°F. Add peppers and bake until skin is blistered, 35-40 minutes. Let cool. Remove peel and seeds and slice pepper into thin strips.

2. In a large bowl, combine lettuce, peppers, tomatoes, cucumbers, mushrooms, and feta cheese.

3. Prepare the dressing: In a jar or blender, combine olive oil, vinegar, honey, mustard, salt, and pepper. Shake well or blend to combine. Drizzle over salad (you will have extra dressing). Toss to combine.

CAESAR SALAD

This is the only hotel restaurant we've included in this book. You'll know why on your next trip to Israel, when you visit (or stay at) David Citadel and sit on the terrace, enjoying the gorgeous view overlooking the walls of the Old City.

And while the hotel is known for its superior ambiance, beauty, location, and service, it's also known for the food. It's well-known that you can get the city's best Caesar salad at David Citadel's Lobby Lounge and Terrace (one of the hotel's four restaurants), which is open from 7 a.m. until 11:30 p.m. The service is fast, the food is tasty, and the restaurant is upscale without being glitzy, making it a perfect place for a business meeting or elegant lunch ... or simply for dining on your own. You'll have the view to keep you company. - L.

DAVID CITADEL
JERUSALEM

DAVID CITADEL

OWNER/CHEF
Executive Chef Itzik Mizrachi

LOCATION
*Jerusalem,
Israel*

ISRAEL

CAESAR SALAD

YIELD *4 servings plus additional dressing*

CATAGORY *dairy*

DESCRIPTION
Romaine lettuce accompanied by croutons, anchovies, Caesar dressing, and Parmesan

Refrigerate remaining dressing for later use. It will keep in the refrigerator for up to 1 week.

INGREDIENTS

1 HEAD	Romaine lettuce, *chopped*
1 CUP	croutons
•	additional anchovies, *if desired*
•	Parmesan cheese, *shaved or grated, for sprinkling*

DRESSING:

4	extra large egg whites
1 TSP	kosher salt
½ TSP	pepper
1	anchovy
1 TBSP	lemon juice
1 TBSP	vinegar
1-2	garlic cloves
2 TBSP	water
1¼ CUPS	oil

INSTRUCTIONS

1. Prepare the dressing: In a food processor, combine egg whites, salt, pepper, anchovy, lemon juice, vinegar, garlic, and water. Blend while slowly drizzling in the oil, until emulsified. You can also combine all ingredients in a jar and use an immersion blender to emulsify.

2. In a large bowl, combine lettuce, croutons, anchovies, if using, and Parmesan cheese. Toss with some of the dressing.

CALIFORNIA SALAD

RESTAURANT • CAFÉ

RIMON BISTRO

LOCATION
Off Ben Yehudah Street in Jerusalem, Israel

ISRAEL

Rimon operates three restaurants in Jerusalem. The first two locations, Rimon Bistro (the meat restaurant) and Café Rimon (the dairy restaurant) are neighbors just off Ben Yehudah Street. The second Rimon Café is located in the Mamilla Mall.

The most amazing thing about Rimon Bistro is that it's open 24 hours a day, 6 days a week, from Motza'ei Shabbos to Erev Shabbos, and the vast majority of the large menu (which is continually updated) is available during all those hours.

Even if it's the middle of the night, your food will be fresh. The busy restaurants have very high turnover, so everything is continuously prepared fresh for the next batch of diners.

Check out the recipe from Rimon Bistro's sister, Café Rimon, on page 194. -L.

CALIFORNIA SALAD

YIELD *2-4 servings*

CATEGORY *meat*

DESCRIPTION

Mixed greens topped with seared turkey and a creamy ginger dressing

Rimon has been in existence for 60 years and is considered a landmark by Jerusalemites.

INGREDIENTS

TURKEY:

2 Tbsp	olive oil
1	*(1-1¼ lb)* skinless and boneless turkey breast
5	garlic cloves, *minced*
2	pinches cumin
5 Tbsp	soy sauce
1 tbsp	*(scant)* brown sugar
1 tsp	tomato paste
1 tsp	kosher salt
½ tsp	crushed black pepper

SALAD:

4 cups	mixed greens
½	red cabbage, *shredded*
1 cup	cherry tomatoes, *halved*
1 small	red onion, *thinly sliced*
1	cucumber, *thinly sliced*
10	mini Israeli pickles, *diced*
¼ cup	peanuts, *coarsely chopped*

DRESSING:

4 TBSP	mayonnaise
1 TSP	fresh grated ginger
2 TBSP	sweet chili sauce
2 TSP	toasted sesame oil
2 TSP	vinegar
2	garlic cloves, *minced*
2 TBSP	water, *as needed for thinning*
½ TSP	kosher salt
⅛ TSP	coarse black pepper

INSTRUCTIONS

1 Preheat oven to 400°F.

2 Prepare the turkey: Heat olive oil in a skillet over medium heat. Add turkey and cook for 3 minutes on each side, until a crust forms. Add garlic and cumin and cook for 1 additional minute. Add soy sauce, brown sugar, tomato paste, salt, and pepper; stir. Bring to a boil.

3 Remove skillet from heat and transfer contents to a baking pan (alternatively, bake in the skillet). Cover with foil and bake for 35 minutes, basting with the sauce periodically. Let cool.

4 Slice turkey into thin slices and return to pan until ready to serve.

5 Prepare the dressing: In a jar, combine mayonnaise, ginger, sweet chili sauce, sesame oil, vinegar, garlic, water, salt, and pepper. Cover and shake until smooth and creamy.

6 In a large bowl, combine greens, cabbage, tomatoes, red onion, cucumber, and pickles. Toss with dressing. Top with turkey slices and peanuts.

HOUSE SALAD

RED HEIFER

OWNER/CHEF
Owner Yosef Wuensch

LOCATION

On King David Street in Jerusalem, Israel

Red Heifer is considered Israel's best American-style steakhouse. It's a modern restaurant, and though the atmosphere feels casual, the food is well presented. Red Heifer is known for its steaks (which are aged for 28 days), appetizers, and really, really good salads.

Favorites from the steak menu include the Red Heifer Classic Rib Eye or the Grand Butterfly (the best steak on the menu). Or get the Red Heifer Burger (with a side of really good fries or even better onion rings) or the Slow-Braised Brisket Sandwich.

No matter what you order for your main, though, this House Salad is the dish people are talking about when they say the Red Heifer has those "really, really good" salads.

It's one of the standouts of the meal. And that's not an easy accomplishment when it's followed by a steak. - L.

HOUSE SALAD

YIELD *2-4 servings*

CATEGORY *meat*

DESCRIPTION

House salad featuring seasonal ingredients and topped with grilled marinated chicken

Owner Yosef Wuensch is no stranger to the restaurant business. He is also an co-owner, with his brother Zalman, of Wolf & Lamb, located at 10 E. 48th Street in Manhattan and in Brooklyn, in a landmark building on Coney Island Avenue (see page 258). He began his career in food by working in a Brooklyn butcher shop. He went on to earn a culinary degree and opened Wolf & Lamb in New York City 17 years ago.

INGREDIENTS

2 TBSP	oil
2	garlic cloves, *crushed*
2 TSP	fresh chopped basil
2 TBSP	lemon juice
1-2	skinless and boneless chicken breasts
1	red pepper
1	yellow pepper
8 OZ	mushrooms, *quartered*
¼ CUP	red wine
¼ CUP	soy sauce
1 HEAD	Romaine lettuce, *chopped*
3 OZ	thinly sliced pastrami

DRESSING *See facing page.*

Red Heifer oftens adds a seasonal vegetable, such as grilled zucchini or eggplant, to this salad.

INSTRUCTIONS

1 In a bowl, combine oil, garlic, basil, and lemon juice. Add chicken and marinate for at least 10 minutes.

2 Meanwhile, preheat oven to 400°F. Roast peppers for 35 minutes, until skin is blistered all around. Let cool; remove and discard peel and seeds. Slice peppers; set aside.

3 In a small bowl, toss mushrooms with red wine, and soy sauce. Let marinate for at least 10 minutes.

4 Preheat a grill or grill pan. Remove chicken from marinade; discard marinade. Add chicken to grill and cook for 3-4 minutes per side. Do not move chicken while cooking and be careful not to overcook it. Set aside. Add mushrooms and cook until soft, about 8 minutes.

5 Prepare the white wine dressing: In a food processor, blend together mayonnaise, Riesling, basil, oregano, garlic, olive oil, onion, lemon juice, salt, and pepper.

6 To serve, in a large bowl, combine lettuce, roasted peppers, and mushrooms. Toss with white wine dressing. Slice chicken into strips. Top salad with chicken strips and pastrami. Drizzle with additional dressing.

WHITE WINE DRESSING:

1 CUP	mayonnaise
¾ CUP	Emerald Riesling Wine or Chardonnay (*add a bit of sugar as this option is less sweet*)
1 TBSP	fresh basil
1½ TSP	oregano
1 TSP	crushed garlic
½ TBSP	olive oil
½ SMALL	onion, *cut into chunks*
1 TBSP	freshly squeezed lemon juice
1 TSP	kosher salt
•	pinch coarse black pepper

More and more chefs today are recommending natural range-fed beef vs. corn-fed beef. Most range-fed beef from America needs more loving care. At Red Heifer, we age our meat for 28 days. For the everyday home chef who wants to use natural beef, I recommend buying your meat early (7 days before use) and keeping it in the coldest section of the fridge (at or below 41°F or 5°C). Slice your steak and marinate in a mixture of teriyaki sauce, wine, and garlic or garlic-infused olive oil and a bit of pineapple juice. Seal tightly. When ready to cook, heat your grill to the maximum. Place steaks on grill and let cook. Don't touch until sweating appears on the steak. Turn and cook to desired temperature. Don't over-cook — overcooked meat is not softer. Bon appetit."

-YOSEF WUENSCH, RED HEIFER STEAKHOUSE

DEVILED KALE SALAD

MASON & MUG

MASON & MUG

OWNER/CHEF
*Co-Owner Sasha Chack /
Chef Itta Werdiger Roth*

LOCATION
*The Prospect
Heights
neighborhood
of Brooklyn,
New York*

For Itta Werdiger Roth, this restaurant serving small plates of global street food is the fitting place to land.

As a former personal chef and line cook at Pardes (see page 250), Itta launched The Hester, the well-known kosher supper club, which she hosted in her living room on a monthly basis (21 times in total). Hester events would always be booked to capacity and she had to move out all her furniture every month to set up the restaurant. On those nights, she'd serve her guests a four-course meal that tapped the limits of her imagination, featuring seasonal produce and unusual flavor pairings.

Then Hester fan (and now business partner) Sasha Chack, who had a background in food and hospitality, approached Werdiger Roth with his idea for his Small Plates, Beer, & Wine Bar.

Then came Mason & Mug, a really fun place. The portions are small, but the prices are too, so you can order a variety or just grab a bite or a snack with your drink.

The vegetarian menu changes every day, but the favorites, like this Deviled Kale Salad, reappear often. We've also heard raves about the cheese plate, their signature bagel & lox sandwiches (with house-cured gravlax), and the "cheese burger" (a stuffed portobello mushroom on a pretzel bun … I want that one). -V.

DEVILED KALE SALAD

YIELD *4-6 servings*

CATEGORY *pareve*

DESCRIPTION

Kale with roasted kabocha squash

Chef Itta advises, "If your oven is tiny and pathetic, like ours at Mason & Mug (even though we are very grateful for it), you might want to roast the squash one tray at a time to avoid it steaming rather than roasting."

INGREDIENTS
SALAD:

1	kabocha squash, *seeded and diced, skin on*
2 Tbsp	olive oil
¼ cup	sesame seeds
5	eggs
•	pinch kosher salt
2	bunches green curly kale, *washed, leaves stripped from stems and spun dry*

DRESSING:

¼ cup	dried seaweed *(hijiki, arame, wakame, or kombu), chopped*
2 cups	rice wine vinegar
1 cup	red miso paste
•	olive oil, *as needed*
7-inch	piece horseradish root, *peeled and finely grated*
•	kosher salt or soy sauce *(if needed)*

INSTRUCTIONS

1. Prepare the squash: Preheat oven to 400°F. Line two baking sheets with parchment paper. Toss squash in olive oil and sesame seeds and spread out over the two trays. Roast until brown and crispy, 35-40 minutes.

2. Prepare the eggs: Place eggs in a single layer in a small saucepan. Add water to just cover; add salt. Bring to a rolling boil. Turn off heat and let eggs sit in water until cool enough to peel. Slice eggs in half.

3. Prepare the dressing: Place the seaweed into a small pot and cover with rice wine vinegar. Bring to a boil and turn off heat. Let seaweed rehydrate and soften in the hot vinegar.

4. In a small bowl, whisk together miso paste and enought olive oil to loosen miso. Add horseradish, cooled seaweed, and some of the rice vinegar, until dressing has the thickness of mayonnaise. Taste; add more salt or soy sauce if necessary.

5. To serve, place the kale into a large mixing bowl and add a few big spoonfuls of dressing. Using your hands, massage the dressing into the kale leaves; transfer the leaves to a serving bowl. Top with roasted kabocha and halved eggs. Finish with a small dollop of the dressing on the bright yolk of each halved egg.

CLOSER LOOK *There are lots of types of seaweed. We used the nori we had in the pantry (usually used for making sushi). Large varieties of seaweed, like wakame or kombu, also need to be rough chopped or thinly sliced into strips. Hijiki, a grass-like seaweed, needs to be pre-soaked before use.*

"Tips? Hmmm ... when you're cooking, try and work around what looks gorgeous when you're shopping or what you already have in the fridge. Don't ever follow a recipe exactly (except when you're baking a cake!). Adjust things the way you (think) you might like them. This way of thinking also avoids wastage of fresh produce."

-CHEF ITTA, MASON & MUG

The same year that Mason & Mug opened, both partners welcomes new babies into their families.

HEIRLOOM TOMATO SALAD

RARE BISTRO

OWNER/CHEF
Owner Baruch Sandhaus

LOCATION
Miami Beach, Florida

If you haven't been to 41st Street in Miami Beach recently, you'll find a kosher culinary renaissance next time you visit. It's due to the vision of restaurateur Baruch Sandhaus. Start in the east and walk west and you'll first pass House of Dogs (that's where I go when I land in Miami after 10 p.m.). Walk a little further and you'll pass Beyond by Shemtov's (see page 206).

A jewel of the Rare Restaurant Group is Rare Bistro, hidden inside Tower 41, a residential tower on the corner of 41st Street and Pinetree Drive. Inside you'll find a refreshing combination of elevated food in a family-friendly atmosphere. Rare Bistro succeeds in pleasing everyone: both the kids who want simple and fun fare, and the adults who want to experience the finest of Miami's culinary offerings (Want more? See page 209).

That vision is further exemplified through the culinary feats of Extreme Catering, the restaurant group's catering arm. Sandhaus is now taking his vision north to Surfside's Harding Avenue, to create two more inspired restaurants: a BBQ spot specializing in slow-cooked smoked meats, as well as the first kosher venture in molecular gastronomy. Rare dining is exciting … and rivals anything you'd find in New York.

This refreshing Heirloom Tomato Salad reminds of us our Rare experience: sublimely elegant, with the flavor of vacation.

With food so good on that vacation, though, don't forget to get some time on the boardwalk. - L.

HEIRLOOM TOMATO SALAD

YIELD *6 servings*

CATEGORY *pareve*

DESCRIPTION

Tomatoes, avocado, and sprouts tossed with a honey vinaigrette and served over watermelon

Save this recipe for the summertime, when both watermelon and tomatoes are at their peak sweetness.

INGREDIENTS

3 CUPS	assorted sprouts *(sunflower sprouts, alfalfa sprouts, bean sprouts) OR microgreens*
3	avocados, *scooped into small balls using a melon baller*
1	English cucumber, *peeled, seeded, and diced*
3-4 SMALL	to medium heirloom tomatoes, *assorted colors, cut into wedges*
6	*(6 x 1½ x 1½ in)* slices seedless watermelon

DRESSING:

1 TBSP	chopped mixed fresh herbs *(Italian parsley, Thai basil, and thyme)*
3 TBSP	extra virgin olive oil
3 TBSP	aged balsamic vinegar
3 TBSP	wildflower honey
•	kosher salt
•	freshly ground black pepper

INSTRUCTIONS

1 In a medium bowl, gently toss together sprouts, avocado, cucumber, and tomatoes.

2 Prepare the dressing: In a small bowl, whisk together fresh herbs, olive oil, balsamic vinegar, honey, salt, and pepper. Pour over sprouts mixture and toss to coat evenly. Taste and adjust seasoning if needed.

3 To serve, plate one slice of watermelon per person and top with salad just before serving.

CLOSER LOOK *Exotic honey can be a chef's secret ingredient. Like wine, the flavor of honey is determined by the terroir (from the French word for earth), a set of characteristics including geography, climate, soil, and temperature that give each honey its complex and individual flavor. For more on wildflower honey, see page 15.*

QUINOA AND SPINACH SALAD

SOYO

OWNER/CHEF

*Owner Lee Landau /
Chef Elad Asnafi*

LOCATION

*Jerusalem, Israel;
London, England*

SOYO is a funky, hip, and fun place to eat, with a health-conscious menu that really lets you customize your meal (pick and choose different options for your salad, sandwich, pasta, breakfast, drink, or sweets). It's a sister to the popular dairy PIZAZA café (which follows the same customization ethos).

It attracts a young and vibrant crowd, and you might want to go for lunch, because in the evening, it can be hard to get a seat (you can make reservations). A new SOYO Jerusalem location has been launched that features the same light and healthy fare, where you can watch your food being prepped indoors or enjoy the ample deck seating outdoors.

Yes, you can make decisions when ordering from the menu. Your food will come exactly as you like it. But if you find making decisions difficult, you can order one of the popular no-decisions-necessary items, like this Quinoa and Spinach Salad. -L.

QUINOA AND SPINACH SALAD

YIELD *4 servings*

CATEGORY *pareve*

DESCRIPTION

Quinoa, spinach, tomato, green beans, sweet potato, red onion, & beets, served with an olive oil & herb dressing

Restaurants prep all their ingredients at the beginning of the day, so it's easy to toss each salad together upon order. But it's not so practical for home cooks to boil, roast, and steam different ingredients for one salad. To avoid using another pot, home cooks can try the quickie method of steaming green beans: place them in a dish with a couple of teaspoons water. Microwave for 1-2 minutes.

INGREDIENTS

SALAD:

¾ CUP	quinoa
1	sweet potato, *peeled and diced*
1 MEDIUM	beet, *peeled and diced*
1 TBSP	olive oil
8 OZ	baby spinach, *roughly chopped*
½	red onion, *finely diced or thinly sliced*
¼ LB	green beans, *lightly steamed, roughly chopped*
½ CUP	cherry tomatoes, *halved*
3 TBSP	sunflower seeds

DRESSING:

1 TBSP	Dijon or yellow mustard
1 TSP	brown sugar
1 TSP	honey
⅓ CUP	olive oil
½ CUP	fresh basil, *loosely packed*
1	garlic clove
1 TSP	kosher salt

INSTRUCTIONS

1. Preheat oven to 400°F.

2. In a medium pot, bring water to a boil. Add quinoa, lower heat, and simmer for 15 minutes, or until the germ separates from the seed. Strain if necessary.

3. Place sweet potato and beet on a baking sheet and toss with olive oil. Bake until soft, about 30 minutes. Let cool.

4. In a large bowl, combine quinoa, sweet potato, beets, spinach, red onion, green beans, and tomatoes.

5. Prepare the dressing: In a small bowl, combine mustard, brown sugar, honey, olive oil, basil, garlic, and salt. Use an immersion blender to blend until smooth. Toss with salad. Top with sunflower seeds and serve.

SOYO chefs cook the quinoa with a touch of cumin and bay leaves to capture true Mediterranean flavors.

SOYO chefs also recommend giving this recipe a twist by using dried apricots instead of cherry tomatoes.

TACO SUPREME SALAD

THE UPPER CRUST

LOCATION
Cedarhurst, New York

NEW YORK

My niece Batya works on Central Avenue in the Five Towns. When I was in the neighborhood for a food demonstration, I stepped into the store to say hello and get restaurant recommendations. While I took notes, the employees crowded around, telling me which dish they love at their favorite restaurants.

It was really clear that The Upper Crust is held in high regard (it shares an owner with another Five Towns favorite, Carlos & Gabby's, featured on page 136). While the specialty brick-oven pizza is authentic and amazing (the pizza maker is from Sicily … you'll get perfectly thin crust that highlights the flavorful toppings, including the house-made fresh mozzarella), it's the creativity of the entire menu that gets all Long Islanders excited to eat there. So, what do the ladies order for lunch? For Batya's co-worker, it's the Cara Mia Salad, but Batya strongly advocated for her favorite, the Taco Supreme Salad, a fun, crunchy, and interesting party of ingredients. And here it is. - V.

TACO SUPREME SALAD

YIELD *4-6 servings*

CATEGORY *dairy*

DESCRIPTION

A fun Mexican-inspired salad with soy meat and crunchy nachos, tossed in a ranch dressing

Soy-based meat substitutes should be located next to the tofu at most supermarkets. We used Light Life's Smart Ground. You can make a meat version of this recipe using ground beef; simply omit the cheese.

INGREDIENTS

1 HEAD	Romaine lettuce, *chopped*
1	avocado, *chopped*
1	jalapeño pepper, *seeds and membranes removed, thinly sliced*
1	red onion, *thinly sliced*
1	tomato, *chopped*
1 CUP	black olives, *sliced*
3 OZ	shredded cheddar cheese

SOY CRUMBLE:

2 TBSP	olive oil
6 OZ	soy meat or chopped soy burger
1 TSP	cumin
1 TSP	chili powder

NACHO CHIPS:

2 OZ	lasagna noodles, *prepared according to package instructions*
¼ CUP	flour
¼ CUP	semolina flour *(see note)*
•	oil, *for frying*

RANCH DRESSING
see facing page

INSTRUCTIONS

1. Prepare the soy crumble: Heat olive oil in a skillet over medium heat. Add soy meat and season with cumin and chili powder. Cook until browned, about 4 minutes. Set aside.

2. Prepare the nacho chips: Combine flour and semolina flour in a shallow dish. Cut cooked lasagna noodles horizontally into strips; dredge in flour mixture, shaking off excess. Heat oil in a small saucepan. When oil is hot, add lasagna strips and fry until golden and crunchy. Set aside. These chips can be prepared in advance.

3. Prepare the dressing: In a blender or mini food processor, combine mayonnaise, shallot, mustard, vinegar, sugar, celery seed, salt, and pepper. Blend until smooth.

4. Assemble the salad: In a large bowl, combine lettuce, avocado, jalapeño, red onion, tomato, and olives. Top with soy crumble and cheddar cheese. Toss with dressing and top with nacho chips.

RANCH DRESSING:

½ CUP	low-fat mayonnaise
1	shallot, *chopped*
2 TSP	Dijon mustard
1 TBSP	vinegar
1 TSP	sugar
¼ TSP	celery seed
1½ TSP	kosher salt
•	pinch white pepper

TIDBIT *The Upper Crust operates in the space that used to be Zomick's Bakery, a favorite local bakery in the Five Towns and beyond for nearly three decades. The Upper Crust probably makes the one dough Zomick's Bakery never made: pizza dough!*

CLOSER LOOK

Semolina is a coarse flour that's commonly used to make pasta. It has a texture similar to cornmeal (which would work fine as a substitute when making these nachos). And like cornmeal, it gives great texture to pizza crust (see page 233). In other Jewish ethnic cuisines, semolina flour is used to make couscous and the dough for the Syrian pastry sambousak.

CAULIFLOWER & CHICKPEA SALAD

TRATTORIA
חבה
יפו 119

TRATTORIA HABA

OWNER/CHEF
Owner The Haba Family /
Chef Michael Katz

LOCATION

ISRAEL

On Rechov Yafo in Machane Yehudah, Jerusalem, Israel

For many years, the Haba family had been operating local bakeries, producing pita breads, challah, Oriental-style breads, cakes, and pastries. Much of their business took place at the famous Jerusalem shuk, Machane Yehudah.

As Machane Yehudah transformed from a place where the local community shops to an international culinary shopping destination, the Haba family envisioned a restaurant that would bring those ingredients into one dining experience.

But how does a family of bakers find success with food?

By teaming up with one of Israel's most prominent chefs, Chef Michael Katz. Trattoria Haba, on Rechov Yafo, is a pretty oasis from the busy market. But if you don't want to leave the market, you can sit at the bar and people-watch. - L.

CAULIFLOWER & CHICKPEA SALAD

YIELD *4 servings*

CATEGORY *dairy*

DESCRIPTION

Chickpeas, spinach, pan-fried cauliflower, kalamata olives, and roasted tinkerbell peppers in a shallot vinaigrette, topped with shavings of caprino cheese

Didn't soak your dried chickpeas overnight? This quickie pre-soaking method will work just as well. Bring a pot of water to a boil. Add chickpeas and boil for 2 minutes. Turn off heat and let sit for 1 hour. Drain. Add 5 cups fresh water and return to a boil. Cook until soft, about 1 hour, as directed.

INGREDIENTS

1 CUP	dried chickpeas
¼ TSP	baking soda
12	mini peppers
½ CUP	olive oil, *plus more to coat peppers*
1 MEDIUM	head cauliflower, *broken into florets*
1 TSP	kosher salt
10 OZ	baby spinach leaves
•	sea salt
•	pepper
½ CUP	kalamata olives, *pits removed*
3 OZ	caprino or Parmesan cheese OR 1/3 cup grated Parmesan

SHALLOT VINAIGRETTE:

2	shallots
3 TBSP	balsamic vinegar
3 TBSP	sherry or red wine vinegar
3 TBSP	water
•	pinch kosher salt
•	pinch coarse black pepper
•	pinch sugar
⅓ CUP	corn oil
⅓ CUP	olive oil, *or to taste*

INSTRUCTIONS

1. Prepare the chickpeas: Soak chickpeas in water overnight with the baking soda. Drain, rinse, and place into a pot with 5 cups fresh water. Bring to a boil and cook over low heat until soft, about 1 hour. Drain and set aside to cool.

2. Prepare the peppers: Preheat oven to 475°F. Lightly grease peppers with olive oil and place on a baking sheet. Roast for 15-18 minutes, or until peppers are soft. Set aside to cool.

3. Prepare the cauliflower: In a saucepan, bring 5 cups water to boil with 1 teaspoon salt. Add cauliflower and blanch until soft but still al dente. Drain and place cauliflower into ice water to stop the cooking process. Pat dry. (You can skip this step if using thawed frozen cauliflower.)

4. Heat olive oil in a frying pan over medium heat. Add cauliflower and pan-fry until golden brown. Lightly season with sea salt.

5. Prepare the vinaigrette: In a blender, combine shallots, vinegars, and water. Blend to a smooth paste. Add salt, pepper, and sugar. Taste and adjust seasoning if necessary. Whisk in oils.

6. To serve, in a large bowl, toss spinach leaves with salt, pepper, and a little dressing (you will have extra dressing). Place leaves in the center of each plate; top with chickpeas, peppers, cauliflower, and olives. Shave cheese directly over salad.

CHEF MICHAEL'S 5 TIPS FOR THE HOME COOK

Remember — hot and dry does not stick! If you want your pan to fry a nice piece of fish without losing the skin, make sure your pan is hot. Pat fish dry and let it stand at room temperature, uncovered, for a few minutes. Add a little bit of butter or olive oil to the pan and gently slide in the fish, skin side down. You will achieve nice, crispy skin.

Mix different lettuce leaves in your salad. I like to combine hard leaves, like iceberg or endives, with more delicate leaves.

Do you love parsley? Chop a large amount. After washing, place in a towel and squeeze out all the water. It will last 3-5 days refrigerated in an airtight container or freeze in a resealable plastic bag.

Pizza dough freezes great! Make the largest amount you can. After the first rise, divide into 8-ounce balls and freeze in lightly oiled plastic bags. Defrost slowly in the refrigerator or at room temperature.

It's better to buy good but inexpensive knives that you will use a lot and replace when they're no longer sharp vs. buying an expensive knife you won't want to replace.

ROCKPORT SALAD

MILK STREET CAFÉ

OWNER/CHEF
*Owner Marc Epstein /
Chef Laura McDaniel*

LOCATION
Boston, Massachusetts

Milk Street Café is the Boston corporate world's answer to lunch. The most well-known kosher restaurant in Boston is also the only kosher restaurant downtown (other kosher restaurants are all in Boston's Brookline neighborhood).

Surrounded by skyscrapers, Milk Street Café has all the neighborhood's employees, not just the kosher ones, looking forward to their lunch break. They crave the soups (Tuscan White Bean in the winter, Watermelon Gazpacho in the summer), pizzas (with toppings like goat cheese and basil), signature sandwiches (the Roasted Tomato Sandwich is a favorite), and this Rockport Salad. The desserts are also popular, including the giant chocolate chip cookie, a fan favorite. Be aware, though: Once the lunch crowd departs, Milk Street closes for the day at 3 p.m.

Need food for the office staff on your schedule? A large part of Milk Street's business is corporate catering (the catering department has both meat and dairy menus), so Boston's busy bees don't even need to leave the office to eat. That's the way a boss can pamper his employees or a prospective client. -V.

ROCKPORT SALAD

YIELD *4 servings*

CATEGORY *dairy*

DESCRIPTION

Pears, red grapes, goat cheese, dried cranberries, pistachios, mixed greens with a honey-balsamic dressing

Chefs cook quickly by always having make-ahead components, like salad dressings, ready. Keep this dressing in the fridge to toss on any salad featuring in-season fruit.

INGREDIENTS

6 OZ	mixed greens
1	pear, *cut into ½-in cubes or sliced*
¾ CUP	red grapes, *halved*
½ CUP	dried cranberries
½ CUP	shelled pistachios
3 OZ	goat cheese, *crumbled*

HONEY-BALSAMIC DRESSING:

2 TBSP	balsamic vinegar
¼ CUP	white vinegar
¼ CUP	honey
½ TSP	lemon juice
½ TSP	coarse sea or kosher salt
⅛ TSP	ground black pepper
6 TBSP	extra virgin olive oil

INSTRUCTIONS

1 In a mixing bowl, combine greens, pears, grapes, cranberries, and pistachios.

2 Prepare the dressing: In a medium bowl, whisk together vinegars, honey, lemon juice, salt, and pepper. Continue to whisk while drizzling in olive oil until dressing is emulsified. Drizzle dressing over salad (you will not need all the dressing) and toss to combine; alternatively, you can serve the dressing on the side.

3 Place salad on each plate and top with goat cheese.

TIDBIT *Although Milk Street Café is a strictly kosher restaurant, it services the entire downtown area of Boston. Over 90 percent of the customers aren't even Jewish.*

"Enjoy the process and journey each dish unfolds. Do not be intimidated and do not overthink. Cooking is artistry at its finest and you get to create beautiful masterpieces. Build a strong foundation of knowledge and skill and keep practicing and exploring. Soon everything will flow together and your end result will be something delicious."

—EXECUTIVE CHEF LAURA McDANIEL,
MILK STREET CAFÉ

BARBECUE TIME

SALADS

Heirloom Tomato Salad
(page 102)

California Salad
(page 90)

SIDES

Sweet Pickles
(page 56)

Guacamole and Chips
(page 22)

ON THE GRILL

Beef Tinga Sliders
(page 40)

Honey-Mustard Hanger Steak
(page 160)

The Belt
(page 140)

SWEET ENDING

Zeppoli Cinnamon
Doughnuts with Chocolate
Dipping Sauce
(page 266)

DAIRY BRUNCH/ LUNCHEON

Deviled Kale Salad
(page 98)

Caesar Salad
(page 87)

Quinoa and Spinach
Salad
(page 106)

Cauliflower &
Chickpea Salad
(page 114)

Vegetable and
Feta Cheese Focaccia
(page 236)

Spinach Quiche
(page 240)

SWEET

Praline Brownies with
Assorted Toppings
(page 272)

MAIN DISHES

EGGPLANT CHICKEN IN GARLIC SAUCE

SEGAL'S OASIS GRILL

OWNER/CHEF
Owner Daniel Gilkarov

LOCATION
Phoenix, Arizona

W hen Leah and I first discussed writing a restaurant cookbook, the first thought that came to my mind was, "The eggplant from Segal's."

My last vacation-sans-kids was quite a while ago. I might have forgotten what the view of the Grand Canyon looks like before I'd forget the dish I enjoyed for dinner during my first night in Arizona.

I had called the chef over to talk about it. And while my husband complimented him on the ribs, I interrupted and said, "That didn't taste like regular eggplant. What was that?"

Like many out-of-town restaurants, Segal's is a casual spot that serves some American, some Chinese, and some Middle Eastern food. There's a sushi menu and a deli menu. But the difference is that it's all really, really good. My husband has returned to Phoenix on business a few times since and Segal's remains the nightly stop.

I had originally ordered the vegetarian version, served with firm tofu (prepare using the same method as the chicken; see note). Try the chicken version for a family-favorite dinner. - V.

EGGPLANT CHICKEN IN GARLIC SAUCE

YIELD *2 servings*

CATEGORY *meat*

DESCRIPTION

Lightly fried chicken and eggplant wokked in a dark and spicy garlic sauce

Segal's was originally a butcher shop. Back in 1967, Zalman and Pearl Segal moved to Phoenix, making kosher food available for the first time in that city. The Segal family sold the business to the Gilkarovs in 2006.

INGREDIENTS

1 LB	eggplant, *cut into 1½-inch chunks*
•	kosher salt, *for sprinkling*
1 LB	skinless boneless chicken breasts, *cut into bite-sized pieces*
3 TBSP	cornstarch, *for dredging*
3 TBSP	chopped garlic
¼ TSP	chili pepper flakes
⅓ CUP	shredded carrots
•	canola or vegetable oil, *for frying*

DARK SAUCE:

⅓ CUP	low-sodium soy sauce
2 TBSP	sugar
1 TSP	toasted sesame oil
1 TSP	ground black pepper
1 TSP	cornstarch

INSTRUCTIONS

1 Sprinkle eggplant chunks with salt; allow to rest for 20-30 minutes (this process will prevent eggplant from soaking up too much oil during frying). Rinse salt from eggplant and drain well.

2 Meanwhile, prepare the sauce: In a small bowl, whisk together soy sauce, sugar, sesame oil, black pepper, and cornstarch. Set aside.

3 Prepare the chicken: Place cornstarch into a shallow dish; toss the chicken in cornstarch to coat very well.

4 Heat 3-inches oil in a wok or 1-inch oil in a sauté pan over medium heat. Add chicken to hot oil and pan-fry until golden, 2-3 minutes per side. Remove from oil and set aside.

5 Add the eggplant to the same pan and fry until light golden, 2-3 minutes. Remove from oil and set aside. Discard oil, leaving about 1 tablespoon in the wok or pan.

6 Add garlic and chili pepper flakes and stir-fry for about 30 seconds. Return chicken and eggplant to the pan. Add carrots and sauce and stir-fry for 2 minutes, coating all the ingredients well with the sauce.

When you see those tall, skinny Asian or Japanese eggplants in your supermarket or farmer's market toward the end of the summer (when they're grown locally) — grab them and make this dish. Segal's imports Asian eggplants from Japan and they help make this dish extra special.

CLOSER LOOK *At Segal's, this dish can also be ordered with either beef or tofu instead of chicken. For a vegetarian entrée, replace chicken with 1 pound firm tofu cut into 1-inch cubes. You may need to adjust the cooking time specified in Step 4.*

"Of all the rules of the kitchen that I have learned and followed over the years, I feel the most important one is if you enjoy cooking, then you do it right. Try not to cook if in a foul mood. And just have fun."

-DANIEL GILKAROV, SEGAL'S OASIS GRILL

CHICKEN FINGERS + CRANBERRY BBQ SAUCE

Gotham Burger Co.

GOTHAM BURGER

OWNER/CHEF
Co-owner Avi Roth

LOCATION
Teaneck, New Jersey and Upper West Side, Manhattan, New York

NEW JERSEY

NEW YORK CITY

One day, after doing an errand in the area, Leah found herself on Queen Anne Road in Teaneck.

"Quick … I have 45 minutes until I have to leave. Where should I go for lunch?" (with the mission of walking out with a recipe). I remember I had interviewed Avi Roth of Gotham Burger a while ago, so I dug up his cell phone number. - V.

Victoria sent me to the right place. Gotham is a modern yet casual restaurant, where the beef is ground in-house and the burgers are served on a brioche bun. A *saucier* (dedicated chef for making sauces) prepares the special touches that go on the burgers and steak sandwiches. You can also get a pareve shake to complete the experience. The Manhattan location is a lounge-like sports bar where young professionals go to grab a beer and dinner after work.

When I arrived, Avi was in the restaurant, and as soon as I told him about the book, I began looking through the menu. What would I want to include in the book (and eat for lunch)? Would it be the Gotham Wings? Their signature Burger? At last, I decided that a great restaurant book needs a great chicken finger, and so I got to work, dipping Gotham's popular crunchy chicken fingers into every one of the eight choices of dipping sauce, which include Cranberry BBQ, Honey Mustard, Lemon Pepper, Blazing Chipotle, Mango Habañero, Tangy Gold BBQ, Raspberry Chipotle, and Garlic Mayo. I then picked my favorite for you. - L.

CHICKEN FINGERS + CRANBERRY BBQ SAUCE

YIELD *4-6 servings*

CATEGORY *meat*

DESCRIPTION
These fingers are not just big in size but "big" in taste. Crispy coated chicken breast has a great crunch. Serve with our delicious dipping sauce.

The original Gotham Burger Cranberry BBQ sauce recipe makes 5 gallons! Although you'll still need to do a lot of dipping to use up this smaller quantity, we froze it successfully.

INGREDIENTS

2 LB	skinless boneless chicken breast, *cut into finger-like strips (about 3-4 strips per breast)*
½ CUP	flour
¾ TBSP	kosher salt
½ TBSP	coarse black pepper
¼ TBSP	paprika
2	eggs
1-2	drops Tabasco hot sauce
2 CUPS	panko crumbs
1 TSP	parsley flakes
•	pinch kosher salt
•	pinch coarse black pepper

CRANBERRY BBQ SAUCE:

½	*(14-oz)* can whole berry cranberry sauce
2⅔ CUPS	BBQ sauce
3 TBSP	brown sugar
1½ TBSP	teriyaki sauce

INSTRUCTIONS

1 In a shallow dish, combine flour, salt, pepper, and paprika.

2 In a second shallow dish, whisk together eggs and hot sauce.

3 Combine panko crumbs, parsley, salt, and pepper in a third shallow dish.

4 Roll chicken first in flour mixture, then egg wash, then panko crumbs.

5 Heat oil in a deep-fryer or saucepan to between 350°F and 375°F. Add chicken and deep-fry for 3½-4 minutes.

6 Prepare the sauce: In a food processor or using an immersion blender, blend cranberry sauce until smooth. Whisk in BBQ sauce, brown sugar, and teriyaki sauce. Serve alongside chicken fingers.

TIDBIT *It's a happy accident that Gotham Burger can also read: Got Hamburger.*

Avi recommends Open Pit or Bull's-Eye BBQ Sauce.

"Use the freshest possible ingredients, especially the spices. If your spices have been sitting for more than 3 months, it's too long. Buy in smaller quantities."

-AVI ROTH, GOTHAM BURGER

POPCORN CHICKEN

Abigael's KOF K

ABIGAEL'S

OWNER/CHEF
Chef Jeffrey Nathan

LOCATION
Midtown Manhattan, New York

NEW YORK CITY

Though we had both been to Abigael's many times, Leah and I first spent time with Alison and Jeffrey Nathan during a visit to Union Square Farmer's Market (where many Manhattan chefs come to find ingredients to create their in-season specials). It was a real treat to have a culinary tour from the kosher world's most renowned chef. We went from booth to booth as Jeffrey taught us about each item as we passed it. We learned how he'd season fresh strawberries in a strawberry salad, cook down fresh fava beans until they were as smooth as butter to make fava bean hummus, and how he uses his favorite king oyster mushrooms.

After we finished our rounds at the market, it was up to Abigael's for lunch. True to our taste buds, I ordered Smoked Brisket Eggrolls; Victoria had the Spicy Asian Salad with ponzu sauce.

Many restaurants come and go, but Abigael's, in its super-central spot on Broadway near Times Square, has always been at the upper echelon of kosher restaurants. It's also one of the largest kosher restaurants (seating 350), but that doesn't compromise the superior service.

Jeffrey and Alison Nathan (who is also a trained chef) began their culinary careers at cutting-edge restaurants. In 1996, they opened Abigael's, to tons of acclaim, to give kosher diners the opportunity to enjoy innovative food.

Chef Jeff went onto become a James Beard award winner and author of bestselling cookbooks, including *Adventures in Jewish Cooking*. He was the first to introduce lots of trends to the kosher food world, including this signature appetizer. - L.

POPCORN CHICKEN

YIELD *3-4 servings*

CATEGORY *meat*

DESCRIPTION

Fried golden chicken breast, tossed with herbs and lemon-cayenne drizzle

At Abigael's, Chef Nathan makes his hot sauce from scratch. We tested different brands and types to find the closest match. We got the best results when combining Frank's Red Hot Sauce with equal parts Thai hot chili sauce or Buffalo-style wing sauce.

INGREDIENTS

2 LB	skinless boneless chicken breasts or tenders, *cut into bite-sized pieces*
•	canola or peanut oil, *for frying*
1 CUP	white wine
¼ CUP	red wine vinegar
¼ CUP	toasted sesame oil
1 CUP	cornstarch
1 CUP	flour
4	egg whites, *lightly whipped*
½ CUP	hot sauce
3 TBSP	lemon juice
2 TBSP	olive oil
1	bunch chives, *chopped*
2 CUPS	popped popcorn

INSTRUCTIONS

1 In a resealable plastic bag, combine wine, vinegar, and sesame oil. Add chicken and refrigerate for at least 2 hours, and up to 12 hours.

2 Heat oil in a deep fryer or pot to 350°F.

3 Line a baking sheet with a double layer of paper towels. Remove chicken from marinade and place on paper towels to drain. Pat dry. Discard any remaining marinade.

4 In a shallow bowl, combine cornstarch and flour.

5 Dip dry chicken into egg whites, then dredge in cornstarch/flour blend. Carefully drop individual pieces of chicken into hot oil. Fry until crisp and golden on all sides, about 2 minutes. Remove from oil and drain on fresh paper towels.

6 In a medium bowl, combine hot sauce, lemon juice, olive oil, and chives. Add chicken and toss until chicken is well-coated. Place on a platter and garnish with popcorn. Serve immediately.

TIDBIT *The number of products with kosher symbols isn't the same as it was back when Abigael's first opened. Jeffrey has been instrumental in bringing many kosher products, including high-quality prepared stocks and spices and authentic panko crumbs, to market.*

"When you include an ingredient in a dish, ask yourself, 'What am I putting this in there for? Is one bitter? Is one sweet? Does one add crunch? Do I need a red or orange for something to pop?' There has to be a thought process, because you are never eating one element at a time."

- CHEF JEFFREY NATHAN, ABIGAEL'S

For a maximum burst of flavor, cut your chicken very small — literally bite-sized.

THE CEDARHURST SANDWICH

CARLOS & GABBY'S

LOCATION

Five Towns, Brooklyn, Riverdale, Queens, New York; Lakewood, New Jersey

Very often, while telling people about this book, we'd play the "Name That Restaurant" game. They'd name a restaurant and we'd tell them the recipe we were featuring.

If we were anywhere in Long Island (the location of the original Carlos & Gabby's), we'd hear "Carlos & Gabby's" and respond, "Cedarhurst Sandwich." Their eyes would light up and they'd say, "That's the best sandwich on the menu! We go just for that!"

As each new location opened, local residents became very excited. It only took a few days for fans to be buzzing about the Cedarhurst Sandwich there too.

Besides being known for making great sandwiches, Carlos & Gabby's is also one of the few East Coast kosher restaurants where you can enjoy Mexican food, including fresh wraps, salads, burritos, and the popular Five-Alarm Chili. The service is fast, the prices are reasonable, and it's super kid-friendly, making it a great place to take the family. Not many kosher restaurants have so many locations — it's a great testament to Carlos & Gabby's popularity. - L.

THE CEDARHURST SANDWICH

YIELD *1 serving*

CATEGORY *meat*

DESCRIPTION

Batter-dipped chicken breast served on a toasted hoagie with grilled pastrami, caramelized onions, shredded lettuce, ripe tomato, and honey-Dijon dressing

We like our sandwiches with toasted bread. After cutting open, toast bread open side down on a hot grill or open side up in a hot oven.

INGREDIENTS

2	skinless boneless chicken breasts
4 Tbsp	plus 1 tsp *(1½ oz)* cornstarch
3 Tbsp	*(1½ oz)* water
¼ cup	*(1½ oz)* flour
1	egg
1 cup	cornflakes, *slightly crushed*
•	oil, *for frying*
4 oz	pastrami, *thinly sliced*
1	onion, *frenched (thinly sliced vertically)*
1	*(12-in)* Italian or French bread
2	lettuce leaves
1	tomato, *sliced*

HONEY-MUSTARD DRESSING:

1 Tbsp	honey mustard
1 Tbsp	mayonnaise
1 tsp	mustard
1 tsp	honey

INSTRUCTIONS

1 In a shallow bowl, combine cornstarch, water, flour, and egg. Place cornflakes into a second shallow bowl.

2 Dredge chicken in batter, then coat with cornflakes.

3 Heat ½ inch oil in a sauté pan to 300°F. Add chicken and fry until chicken is golden, about 3 minutes per side.

4 Heat a grill or grill pan. Add pastrami and onion slices; cook until pastrami is crisp and onions are soft, about 5-6 minutes.

5 Meanwhile, prepare the honey mustard dressing: In a small bowl, combine honey mustard, mayonnaise, mustard, and honey.

6 Slice bread lengthwise. Layer with chicken cutlets, lettuce, tomato, pastrami, onions, and honey-mustard dressing.

TIDBIT *Carlos & Gabby's is a takeoff of a famous Mexican restaurant in South America called Carlos & Charlie's. While Carlos and Charlie's represents the best of Mexican and American fusion cuisine, Carlos and Gabby's represents the best in Mexican kosher.*

American cooks aren't used to weighing ingredients, but it's a good habit to have. At Carlos & Gabby's, the batter for the chicken is measured by weighing the ingredients in ounces for perfect, consistent results. We included both measurements for your convenience.

THE BELT

SUB EXPRESS

OWNER/CHEF
Owner Ben Grossman

LOCATION
The Borough Park neighborhood of Brooklyn, New York

NEW YORK CITY

There are lots of sandwich shops and fast-food restaurants all over the world — kosher ones too. So why did we choose Sub Express to represent "fast food" in this book? Hands down, Sub Express is where you get the freshest and best kosher sub sandwiches in the Northeast. When we received the recipe, we realized why. Every component is thought through. And while it may seem like work to create each component, one at a time, that's what's necessary to create a sandwich full with flavor that explodes in your mouth.

They have a huge menu, including a variety of cuisines, but I definitely have my favorites: #1 is the Pastrami Sizzlers. One of my favorite sandwiches is The Belt, featured here. My other favorite sandwiches include the Grand Papa (grilled steak slices topped with fried onion, honey BBQ sauce, and Russian dressing) and the Crossfire (grilled pastrami smothered with buffalo-glazed onion rings, coleslaw, and honey-ranch dressing).

There are lots of healthier options on the menu too, plus Mexican dishes, including Taquitos, Chimichanga, and Fajita Nachos. So when you're in the 13th Avenue neighborhood, and you need the best possible food quick, this is where you stop. -L.

THE BELT

YIELD *4 sandwiches*

CATEGORY *meat*

DESCRIPTION

Grilled baby chicken with fried onion and roasted peppers in garlic mayo and pesto sauce.

"The Belt" used to be called "The Belt Parkway," after the Brooklyn highway. It has significance to owner Ben Grossman, as he lives in the Five Towns and spends the greater part of his commute on "The Belt."

INGREDIENTS

PEPPERS, BEFORE ROASTING:

2	red bell peppers
¾ TSP	kosher salt
¾ TSP	black pepper
6 TBSP	olive oil

PEPPERS, AFTER ROASTING:

1 TSP	chopped fresh basil
½ TSP	kosher salt
•	pinch black pepper
¼ CUP	olive oil
2	garlic cloves, *finely diced*

SAUTÉED ONION:

3 TBSP	oil
1	whole Spanish onion, *thinly sliced*

PESTO:

½	bunch fresh basil (*½ cup packed*)
½ CUP	olive oil
2	garlic cloves
1 TSP	pine nuts
1 TSP	kosher salt
•	pinch black pepper

GARLIC MAYO:

1 CUP	mayonnaise
2	garlic cloves
½ TSP	black pepper
1 TSP	sugar
½ TSP	mustard
3 OZ	pickles, *finely diced*

BONELESS DARK CHICKEN:

1 TSP	kosher salt
½ TSP	black pepper
¾ TSP	cumin
¾ TSP	garlic powder
½ TSP	dried rosemary
½ TSP	dried thyme
¾ TSP	sugar
1 TSP	paprika
2 LB	boneless chicken thighs
4	*(8-in)* French baguettes

INSTRUCTIONS

1 Prepare the roasted peppers: Preheat oven to 350°F. Toss whole peppers in salt, pepper, and olive oil. Bake, uncovered, until skin is blistered, about 35 minutes. Place peppers into a bowl and cover with plastic wrap. Let rest, covered, for 20 minutes or until pepper is cold. Remove and discard pepper core, seeds, and skin. Slice pepper into ½ inch strips. Toss strips with basil, salt, pepper, olive oil, and garlic.

2 Prepare the sautéed onion: Heat oil in a sauté pan over medium heat. Add onion and sauté until golden, but still slightly crispy, 7 minutes.

3 Prepare the pesto: In a blender, combine basil, olive oil, garlic, pine nuts, salt, and pepper. Blend until coarsely ground. Set aside.

4 Prepare the garlic mayo: In a blender, combine mayonnaise, garlic, pepper, sugar, and mustard. Blend until smooth. Stir in pickles. Set aside.

5 Prepare the chicken: In a small bowl, combine salt, black pepper, cumin, garlic powder, rosemary, thyme, sugar, and paprika. Sprinkle on chicken; marinate chicken in spices for 10 minutes. Heat a grill or grill pan and grill chicken for 4 minutes on each side.

6 To assemble, slice baguettes lengthwise and toast. Layer chicken, roasted peppers, pesto, onions, and garlic mayo.

We also like this recipe using chicken breast.

CHERMOULA CHICKEN BREAST

THE URBAN GRILL

OWNER/CHEF
Chef Todd Aarons

LOCATION
Mexico City, Mexico

We've never been to Mexico City, but thanks to the Romano family, it's now a destination that has great kosher food. When the restaurateurs planned to open their fine dining establishment, The Urban Grill, they called on Chef Todd Aarons (see page 182). For a year, Chef Todd traveled back and forth from his home to Bosques de las Lomas, Mexico City to make The Urban Grill into a modern New York-style sushi and steakhouse, with a menu that's true to its location (such as Rib Eye Tacos, Eye of the Rib, and Beef and Lamb Sliders). Chef Aarons created the recipes, trained the staff, and continues to guide them in making The Urban Grill a premier dining experience … in a city where you'd least expect it.

Even for those who consider Mexico City their home, a visit to The Urban Grill feels like a getaway with inviting architecture (the outdoor seating is under arches; there's a curved wall of windows overlooking more arches and greenery) and decor (rustic elegance with an exposed brick wall). It's just the place to enjoy this Chermoula Chicken, with its aromatic and exotic marinade. - V.

CHERMOULA CHICKEN BREAST

YIELD *6 servings*

CATEGORY *meat*

DESCRIPTION

Pechuga de pollo con aceite de oliva, jugo de limón, cúrcuma, perejil (Chicken breast with olive oil, lemon juice, turmeric, and parsley)

Chef Todd recommends serving this chicken with bulgur pilaf or couscous and sautéed mushrooms.

INGREDIENTS

6	skinless boneless chicken breasts or airline breasts *(with wing)*
½ CUP	packed fresh cilantro
¼ CUP	fresh parsley leaves
•	zest of 2 lemons
½ CUP	freshly squeezed lemon juice
2 TBSP	fresh minced ginger
6	garlic cloves
1 TBSP	cumin
2 TSP	ground coriander
2 TSP	turmeric
1 TSP	chili flakes (optional, *for spicy version*)
½ CUP	olive or grapeseed oil
1 TSP	kosher salt
•	pinch coarse black pepper

INSTRUCTIONS

1 In a blender or food processor, combine cilantro, parsley, lemon zest, lemon juice, ginger, garlic, cumin, coriander, turmeric, and chili flakes (optional). Blend, streaming oil into mixture until fully incorporated.

2 Transfer mixture to a medium bowl. Add chicken and marinate, in the refrigerator, for at least 2 hours or maximum 1 day.

3 Remove chicken from marinade; discard marinade. Season chicken with salt and pepper.

4 Preheat a grill to medium-high heat. Add chicken and grill, about 7-8 minutes per side.

CLOSER LOOK *Grapeseed oil is popular in restaurant kitchens (it's also used on page 154) because it has a high smoke point of over 450°F, helping cooks avoid burnt oil. It has a very light taste, so it won't overwhelm other ingredients in a salad dressing, and can stand in for either olive oil or vegetable oils. The oil is made from the seeds inside red and green grapes (which are comprised of less than 10 percent oil). Once the winemaking process is complete, the seeds are dried and crushed to extract the oil.*

CLOSER LOOK *Chermoula, a sauce made from herbs and spices, was originally made in North African countries such as Algeria, Morocco, or Tunisia, using a mortar and pestle. And though it's traditionally used as a marinade for fish, you can use it to marinate any type of meat or vegetables too. Consider it North Africa's aromatic version of pesto and use it as a sauce to flavor couscous or rice.*

At The Urban Grill, basil is sometimes used in place of cilantro.

SESAME CHICKEN

KOSHER CHINESE EXPRESS

OWNER/CHEF
Chef Dianfei Jiang

LOCATION
Manalapan, New Jersey

NEW JERSEY

Kosher Chinese Express is kosher's answer to the little Chinese takeout spot, where the wok is always hot and there's not really much room to sit. You can, though, get a lot of authentic American-style Chinese food for not so much money. Kosher Chinese Express, though, is known more for its takeout (it delivers to a really wide radius); you can even affordably cater an all-Chinese food party from the menu (complete with fortune cookies and chow mein noodles).

It's known for good versions of the classics: like this Sesame Chicken, General Tso's Chicken, Beef with Broccoli, Mu Gu Gai Pan, Pu Pu Platters, and perfect Lo Mein. There are also lots of healthy alternatives, like steamed chicken or beef with vegetables (it will still have that velvety texture). -V.

SESAME CHICKEN

YIELD *4 servings*

CATEGORY *meat*

DESCRIPTION

Double-fried dark chicken nuggets, with a sweet and salty glaze, sprinkled with sesame seeds

Kosher Chinese Express is a family business, now in its second generation. The Sesame Chicken has been one of the most popular dishes on the menu for all of the restaurant's 21 years in business.

INGREDIENTS

2 LB	boneless dark chicken thighs, *cut into ½-inch squares*
2 TSP	baking soda
½ TSP	kosher salt
•	pinch coarse black pepper
1	egg white
⅓ CUP	cornstarch
•	oil, *for frying*
•	sesame seeds, *for sprinkling*

SAUCE:

4	garlic cloves, *crushed*
1	scallion, *finely chopped*
½ CUP	water
¾ CUP	low-sodium soy sauce
5 TBSP	sugar
5 TBSP	white or rice vinegar
2 TBSP	cornstarch, *dissolved in ¼ cup water*

INSTRUCTIONS

1. Place chicken into a medium bowl. Add water to cover; add baking soda. Stir; marinate for 1 hour to tenderize. Rinse chicken well.

2. In a medium bowl, combine chicken, salt, pepper, and egg white. Sprinkle in cornstarch and stir to coat the chicken.

3. Heat oil in a wok. When hot, fry chicken in batches, about 3 minutes. Drain each batch as you fry additional chicken. Return each batch to wok and fry again until crispy, 3-4 minutes. Remove chicken and keep warm. Pour off oil from wok, leaving about 1 tablespoon to prepare the sauce.

4. Prepare the sauce: Heat oil in a clean wok over high heat. Add garlic and scallion. Stir for 1-2 minutes, being careful not to burn. Add water, soy sauce, sugar, and vinegar. Bring to a boil and add in cornstarch mixture, cooking until sauce is thick and sticky. Add in chicken and toss to coat. Sprinkle with sesame seeds.

CLOSER LOOK *In place of the soy sauce, the restaurant uses a Chinese "brown sauce," otherwise known as "the mother sauce" or "base sauce." Brown sauce is a American soy-based sauce. It's usually made out of chicken stock and soy sauce, and flavored with aromatics such as garlic and ginger. Light soy sauce is a good replacement in this version. You can make your own by adding 1 teaspoon chopped garlic, 1 teaspoon ginger, 1 chopped scallion, 4 tablespoons dark soy sauce, 2 tablespoons sugar, and 2 tablespoons cooking wine to 1 cup boiling chicken or vegetable stock. Let sit until cool and strain through a sieve.*

To add some spice to your sesame chicken, add some chili oil while sautéing the garlic.

We've also made this using chicken breast.

DUCK WITH SOUR CHERRY REDUCTION

MIKE'S BISTRO

OWNER/CHEF
Owner/Chef Mike Gershkovich

LOCATION
Midtown Manhattan, New York

NEW YORK CITY

"An incredible meal any time."

"Always delicious."

"My favorite place to go in Manhattan."

That's what people say about Mike's Bistro.

It's no wonder, with Chef Mike Gershkovich at the helm, one of the culinary masterminds of the kosher world (for more on Chef Mike, see page 80). Lots of Mike's dishes have reached legendary status: the Braised Short Ribs (preparing them is a three-day process), the Homemade Gnocchi (with duck confit), and Seared Pekin Duck Breast. Diners also rave about the Black Angus Rib Eye or surprising appetizers like the Exotic Mushrooms or Spicy Merguez Dumplings.

Mike's Bistro is a place you feel like coming back to; Chef Mike walks around visiting as many tables as he can to chat about the food. And if you love food, a chat with Mike is fascinating. Just make sure you make your reservation early. -V.

DUCK WITH SOUR CHERRY REDUCTION

YIELD *1 serving*

CATEGORY *meat*

DESCRIPTION

Seared and roasted duck breast with a cherry reduction

Every recipe of Chef Mike's comes with a culinary lesson. With this one, we learned the proper way to prepare delectable duck. He told us, "It's important to note that this duck will not be hot. There's no such thing as rare and hot. When it comes out of the pan, it will be warm."

INGREDIENTS

1 LARGE	duck breast
1 TBSP	grapeseed oil
•	kosher salt, *for sprinkling*
•	black pepper, *for sprinkling*

SOUR CHERRY REDUCTION:

1 CUP	sour cherry juice
¼ CUP	port wine
•	fresh cherries, *halved and pitted, for garnish (optional)*

INSTRUCTIONS

1 Remove duck breast skin and dry breast thoroughly with a paper towel (the drier the duck, the better it will cook).

2 Prepare the sour cherry reduction: In a small saucepan, combine sour cherry juice and port wine. Cook until sauce is extremely concentrated and thick, being careful not to burn.

3 Preheat oven to 500°F.

4 Heat a cast-iron pan on the stove top until hot (with no oil).

5 Brush duck with grapeseed oil and season with salt and pepper. Use a generous amount of pepper, as the duck will be served with a sweet sauce and the pepper will offset the sweetness.

6 Add duck to pan to sear. It should sizzle aggressively. Immediately transfer pan to oven and cook for 3 minutes. Turn duck over and cook an additional 2 minutes. Remove from oven and rest it on a rack. The duck should be cooked rare to medium rare.

7 Slice duck very thinly. Serve with sour cherry sauce and garnish with fresh cherries, if desired.

CLOSER LOOK *Sour cherry juice (touted for its antioxidants) is found in health food stores and in the health food sections of supermarkets. Note that sour cherry juice will take longer to reduce than sour cherry juice concentrate. The result should be the same.*

It was Chef Mike who gave us the initial inspiration for "The Secret Pantry" section on page 14. When we told him we were writing Secret Restaurant Recipes, he said that rather it should be Secret Restaurant Ingredients. Although home cooks still need recipes, we agreed that quality ingredients are the most important part of a good dish.

BRAISED SHORT RIBS

ESTRÉIA

NOUVELLE CUISINE AT RIVER 978

ESTRÉIA

OWNER/CHEF
Chef Aryeh Goldenson

LOCATION
Lakewood, New Jersey

NEW JERSEY

With the opening of Estréia, the culinary scene in Lakewood, NJ did an about-face. Before Estréia, the town was home to a variety of family-friendly restaurants and great takeout options.

Then, all of a sudden, Estréia brought the Manhattan restaurant experience to Lakewood. Entering through the marble vestibule, diners first come to Estréia for fine dining, ambiance, and attentive white-glove service that's closer to home … but they keep coming back once they enjoy the unexpected: some of the best cuts of meat you'll find anywhere. At Estréia, the Cowboy and Tomahawk Steaks are king (although please order them medium-rare).

Start with classic appetizers like Veal Sweetbreads or Tuna Tartare. Entrees such as the Hoisin Duck or the Chimichurri Skirt Steak are popular, but even if you're ordering salmon, you can be sure that your balsamic-glazed pistachio-crusted fillet will be flavorful and cooked perfectly.

The Estréia secret, though, that we were the most eager to learn was the technique they use to get their signature Braised Short Ribs, another super-popular dish, so incredibly soft. And here it is. -L.

BRAISED SHORT RIBS

YIELD 4 servings

CATEGORY meat

DESCRIPTION

Boneless short ribs simmered in apple BBQ sauce and served with mashed Yukon potatoes and crispy onions

The restaurant makes its own version of barbecue sauce, but Chef Aryeh recommends Jack Daniels #7 Sauce for the home cook.

It is preferable to use heavy-duty plastic wrap when using this technique (see page 12). Ordinary plastic wrap can be used, although it does not hold up as well; it will tear easily as you remove it from the pan.

INGREDIENTS

- 4 *(2 x 8-in pieces)* boneless flanken
- kosher salt, *for sprinkling*
- coarse black pepper, *for sprinkling*
- oil, *for sautéing*
- 1½ CUPS barbecue sauce
- 1½ CUPS apple juice

"Season and reseason at every stage of cooking. If you sweat onions, add salt and pepper. When you add other ingredients, add salt and pepper as well. As a chef I always season in layers, adding a little at a time."

- CHEF ARYEH GOLDENSON, ESTRÉIA

INSTRUCTIONS

1 Preheat oven to 300°F. Season flanken with salt and pepper on both sides.

2 Heat oil in a sauté pan over medium-high heat. When oil is hot, add flanken and sear, about 2 minutes per side. Transfer meat to a baking pan.

3 In a small bowl, whisk together barbecue sauce and apple juice. Pour over flanken. Cover baking pan with a double layer of plastic wrap, then cover the plastic wrap with a double layer of aluminum foil. Be sure to crimp the edge of the foil over the plastic wrap, covering it completely to prevent plastic wrap from melting. (This technique will help seal in the moisture; see page 12.)

4 Bake for 3 hours. Remove from oven.

5 Raise oven heat to 375°F. Before serving, brush ribs with a thin layer of additional barbecue sauce and bake, uncovered, for an additional 20-30 minutes. Serve over Yukon Gold mashed potatoes and crispy onions.

YUKON GOLD MASHED POTATOES

3 LB	Yukon Gold potatoes *(with the peel)*, *cut into chunks*
2 TBSP	oil
1	onion, *diced*
5	garlic cloves, *minced*
4 OZ	margarine, *melted*
½ CUP	nondairy creamer
•	kosher salt, *to taste*
•	pinch coarse black pepper, *to taste*

1 Add potatoes to a pot and cover generously with water. Bring to a boil over high heat and boil until potatoes are soft, about 20 minutes. Drain; transfer potatoes to a medium bowl.

2 Meanwhile, heat oil in a sauté pan over medium heat. Add onion and garlic and sauté until onions are golden, about 10 minutes.

3 While potatoes are still warm, mash with margarine and non-dairy creamer. Add onions and garlic and mash until smooth. Season with salt and pepper.

CRISPY ONIONS

1 LARGE	Spanish onion, *thinly sliced and cut into half-moons*
¼ CUP	vinegar
3 TBSP	sugar
½ TSP	kosher salt plus a pinch, *divided*
¾ CUP	flour
•	pinch coarse black pepper
¼ TSP	paprika
•	oil, *for frying*

1 In a medium bowl, combine vinegar, sugar, and pinch salt. Add onion; marinate for 15 minutes.

2 In a shallow bowl, combine flour, ½ teaspoon salt, pepper, and paprika. Dredge marinated onion strips in flour mixture.

3 Heat oil in a deep fryer or saucepan to 350°F. Add onion strips and fry until crispy, about 3 minutes.

HONEY-MUSTARD HANGER STEAK

etc. steakhouse

ETC. STEAKHOUSE

OWNER/CHEF
Chef Seth Warshaw

LOCATION
Teaneck, New Jersey

NEW JERSEY

Etc. Steakhouse's chef and owner won't be found in the front of the house. If you want to pay him a compliment, he'll be back in the kitchen. He opened the restaurant because he wants to cook.

That passion is the same reason you won't find the same menu at each and every visit. Though the favorites will always be there, Chef Seth keeps reinventing the menu to take advantage of each season's most flavorful produce. As a result, every week there will be new dishes, and every eight weeks, the menu will change completely. Yes, it's more work. Great chefs, though, love to create, and that's what keeps diners excited. The restaurant even has its own farm, which ensures that the freshest local flavors make it to the plate.

Can't decide what to order? One of the most special nights at Etc. is when you enjoy one of the multi-course tasting menus, a "must try" if you want to experience the range of Chef Seth's culinary creativity. And if you're a restaurant-goer who needs to finish a meal with a great dessert, at Etc. you'll find an exciting selection that also changes with the seasons.

This Hanger Steak is one of the favorite Etc. Steakhouse entrees — and while the steak might be paired with this Purple Potato Hash in the wintertime, in the summertime, when there's new bounty in season, you can enjoy your steak with an entirely new accompaniments (think roasted garlic spread, fresh spring peas and mint, fig risotto, and a fig balsamic reduction). - V.

HONEY-MUSTARD HANGER STEAK

YIELD *4 servings*

CATEGORY *meat*

DESCRIPTION

Steak served with purple potato hash, runny egg, and maple mustard glaze

At home, Chef Seth's wife is in charge of the kitchen. Besides, cooking in a home kitchen can be frustrating for a chef because, as Chef Seth says, "I don't know why it takes so long for the pan to get hot."

Prepare the runny egg once you flip the steak. Heat a nonstick sauté pan and crack your eggs into it. Don't let the pan get too hot, as you want the whites not to brown and the yolk just set. Remove eggs from the pan and, using a ring mold, cut a circle out of the eggs so you have a small ring of white and the yolk.

INGREDIENTS

2 LB	hanger steak, *tendon removed from the center, cut into 4 (6-oz) pieces*
•	oil
•	kosher salt, *as needed*
•	coarse black pepper, *as needed*
•	olive oil, *as needed*
½ CUP	spicy brown mustard
½ CUP	pure maple syrup

"Just because you are cooking at home doesn't mean you shouldn't take the time to do things right. Don't skimp on the small things, like chicken stock (make your own!). It makes all the difference. Lots of small things add up to one big thing and sometimes that's the success of the dish."

- CHEF SETH WARSHAW, ETC. STEAKHOUSE

INSTRUCTIONS

1 Soak hanger steak in water for several hours, changing the water every half hour (this will remove the saltiness).

2 Remove from water and pat dry.

3 Heat a cast-iron pan or sauté pan. Once pan is hot, add a bit of oil until it smokes just a little. (Alternatively, preheat a grill until very hot).

4 Season steak with salt and pepper. Add to pan, making sure to place the steak away from you so the oil doesn't splatter. Cook for 4-6 minutes per side. (If using a grill, grill meat directly over fire on one side, then finish indirectly over the fire on the other side).

5 Meanwhile, in a small bowl, whisk together mustard and maple syrup. Brush over steak before serving.

6 To plate the complete dish as in the photo, place a ring mold on a plate. Add the hash and push down with a spoon. Remove the ring mold and place the egg on top (see note). Place steak next to hash and sprinkle some of the spice mix on the egg and around the plate.

PURPLE POTATO HASH

- oil, *as needed for sautéing*
- 1 LB mini purple potatoes, *sliced into thin rounds*
- 1 SMALL butternut squash, *peeled, seeded, and finely diced*
- 1 red pepper, *diced*
- 1 yellow pepper, *diced*
- 1 orange pepper, *diced*
- 2 shallots, *diced*
- 2 garlic cloves, *minced*
- 1 TSP onion powder
- 1 TSP garlic powder
- 1 TSP chili powder
- 1 TSP paprika
- kosher salt
- pepper

1 Heat oil in a large sauté pan. Add potatoes and sauté until tender, about 10 minutes. Remove from pan and set aside. Add additional oil if needed before adding next vegetables to the pan. Add butternut squash to the pan and sauté until tender, about 15 minutes. Remove from pan and set aside. Add peppers, shallots, and garlic and sauté until peppers are tender, about 10 minutes. Remove from pan and set aside. Return all vegetables to the pan to warm through.

2 Meanwhile, in a small bowl, combine onion powder, garlic powder, chili powder, and paprika.

3 Season vegetables with salt, pepper, and half of the spice mix (reserve remaining spices to sprinkle over the plated dish).

CLOSER LOOK *What are purple potatoes? While we think they've become popular for their looks, the rise in the demand for purple potatoes might be due to their health content. The color is a hint that these beautiful spuds are rich in the same antioxidants found in berries and pomegranates, along with a host of vitamins and proteins that white-fleshed potatoes can't boast about. They originate from Peru and Bolivia.*

CHEF'S SPECIAL

SHALLOTS BISTRO

SHALLOTS BISTRO

OWNER/CHEF
Executive Chef Carlos Resendiz

LOCATION
Skokie, Illinois

ILLINOIS

When you first walk into Shallots Bistro, Chicago's premier fine-dining restaurant, your first impression will be, "I've come to the right place." The ambiance, with its cultured stone walls and wood-burning fireplace, is striking and intimate.

Shallots is most well known for both incredible sushi and steak.

If you're a sushi lover, you'll be very impressed by the spectacular presentation, creativity, and flavor. With the astonishing variety of sushi options, you can choose to make it your meal (with unique Sushi Tacos or Japanese 7-Spice Ahi Tuna Tataki with wasabi truffle sauce, or just your starter (with Jalapeño Poppers or a selection of Makimono rolls), saving room for one of Shallots' signature steaks.

Time for that steak. The traditional dinner menu is vast for a fine-dining restaurant, with appetizers such as Homemade Gnocchetti (with wild mushrooms and truffle oil), fish entrées including Grapefruit Sea Bass, classic entrées like Pomegranate Glazed Rack of Lamb — or go straight to the steak menu with this Chef's Special. Choose a choice, well-marbled piece of meat, just as Shallots does, and you'll know why this is the right way to enjoy your steak. - **V**.

CHEF'S SPECIAL

YIELD *1 serving*

CATEGORY *meat*

DESCRIPTION

Eye of the rib fillet, served with crispy onion rings and topped with a mushroom-wine reduction

Beer is the ingredient that makes the crust of the onion rings extra crispy; however, the batter must be used right away.

INGREDIENTS

1	*(10-oz)* eye of the rib fillet
2 TSP	olive oil, *plus more for rubbing on steak*
•	kosher salt
•	Cajun spice blend
1 TSP	flour
1 TSP	porcini mushroom powder
8-10	button mushrooms, *quartered*
1 TBSP	minced shallots
¼ CUP	red wine
½ CUP	beef consommé

INSTRUCTIONS

1. Preheat oven to 350°F.

2. Place an oven-proof skillet over medium-high heat. Add 1 tablespoon olive oil.

3. Rub a thin coat of olive oil over the steak. Lightly salt and season the steak with Cajun spice. Gently dust steak with flour and porcini mushroom powder.

4. Add steak to skillet and sear for 3 minutes on each side. Place pan in oven and bake for 10 minutes (for medium-rare).

5. Remove steak from oven and place on a cutting board. Return skillet to the stove at medium heat. Add 1 tablespoon olive oil, mushrooms, and shallots. Sauté until they just begin to soften, 3-4 minutes.

6. Add red wine and reduce for 3 minutes. Add beef consommé and continue to cook until sauce coats the back of a spoon (see page 12). Add salt to taste.

7. Plate steak; pour mushroom sauce over. Top with onion rings.

SHALLOTS' BEER-BATTERED ONION RINGS

At Shallots, this steak is served with lyonnaise potatoes, blanched asparagus, and these beer-battered onion rings.

1 CUP	flour
1 TSP	paprika
1 TSP	ground mustard
1 TSP	finely chopped parsley
½ CUP	lager beer
⅓ CUP	warm water
¾ TSP	kosher salt
•	pinch coarse black pepper
1 LARGE	Spanish onion, *cut into ½-inch-thick rings*
•	oil, *for frying*

1. In a shallow dish, combine flour, paprika, ground mustard, parsley, beer, water, salt, and pepper.

2. Heat oil to 350°F.

3. Coat onion rings in batter. Add to hot oil and fry until golden brown.

Just a sprinkle of porcini mushroom powder adds depth to a steak. For more about porcini powder, see page 15.

"When cooking, sautéing, or searing with butter or margarine, add a little bit of vegetable oil to the pan before the butter; this will prevent the butter from burning on high heat."

- EXECUTIVE CHEF CARLOS RESENDIZ, SHALLOTS BISTRO

CÔTE DE BOEUF

Le Marais ™ ⓤ

LE MARAIS

OWNER/CHEF

Executive Chef and Co-Owner
José de Meirelles

LOCATION

Times Square,
Manhattan,
New York

NEW YORK CITY

Here's something you might not know about me. When I was a teenager, I was vegetarian for six years. Then, I went with a group of friends to Le Marais. One person ordered the Tournedos Steaks with Béarnaise Sauce (a classic French steak dish) for everyone. Everyone else started to eat, while I stared at my steak. Finally someone said, "If you're not going to eat that, I'm going to eat that."

So I dug in. And it was the single most delicious bite I had experienced in a long time. Vegetarian no more. I suppose I had just been waiting for the right kind of meat.

Le Marais is the kind of steakhouse where you'd better order a steak (I have ordered fish there … only to be laughed at by everyone else at the table). Executive Chef José de Meirelles set the bar high for fine kosher dining when he opened the French brasserie-style steakhouse in 1995. He applies his vast knowledge on how to butcher, season, and cook all varieties of meat to both the restaurant and the in-house butcher showcase (you'll pass it on the way to your table), where you can buy premiere aged meats.

Since that visit, I still order the Tournedos (and it's even better when I get a table with one of those comfy leather armchairs), but their signature Côte de Boeuf, a huge hunk of meat, is what makes meat-lovers want to stand up and sing. (Since the restaurant is in the theater district, that might not seem so odd.) - **V**.

CÔTE DE BOEUF

YIELD *2 servings*

CATEGORY *meat*

DESCRIPTION

Prime Rib for Two

Chef José de Meirelles recommends cooking this meat only to the perfect rare to medium rare "that this meat is so deserving of. Above medium rare? Hang your head in shame, you have disgraced the steer and made its existence meaningless." Don't order the Côte de Boeuf well done!

INGREDIENTS

- 2 *(36-oz)* rib eye steaks, *bone in*
- • kosher salt
- • coarse black pepper

CHIMICHURRI SAUCE:

- 6 garlic cloves OR 3 Tbsp roasted garlic purée
- 1 TSP red pepper flakes
- ½ CUP apple cider vinegar
- ½ CUP chopped fresh mint
- ½ CUP chopped fresh flat-leaf parsley
- ½ CUP chopped fresh basil
- ¾ CUP extra virgin olive oil

INSTRUCTIONS

1 Remove steaks from refrigerator and let come to room temperature on the counter for about 1 hour before cooking.

2 Meanwhile, prepare the chimichurri sauce: In a blender, combine garlic, red pepper flakes, vinegar, herbs, and olive oil. Blend until sauce is well combined yet still coarsely textured. Set aside.

3 Preheat a clean grill to medium-high heat and close the lid.

4 Season all sides of steaks with salt and pepper. Using a clean cloth or bunch of paper towels, rub vegetable oil on the grill. Add steaks and cook for 4 minutes without moving them. Then, turn steak 180 degrees to create diamond markings. (Do not move the meat around, as this is the most common mistake made by home grillers.) Repeat on the other side, until steaks are nicely browned on both sides.

5 Remove steaks from grill and lower heat to medium. Return steak to grill and close the lid. Cook for 6 minutes without moving steaks. Flip steaks and cook an additional 6 minutes for medium-rare.

6 Allow steaks to rest on a cutting board for 10 minutes before slicing. Serve with chimichurri sauce.

TIDBIT *Le Marais is named after the Parisian district that has been associated with the Jewish quarter for centuries. The district is also the historic home of the aristocracy, as the kings of the Ancien Regime maintained their residences in the area. The Jewish quarter, in the 4th arrondissement, is centered around rue de Rosiers ("street of the rosebushes"). Today, the neighborhood is where you'll find kosher restaurants, groceries, Judaica, and upscale clothing shops.*

Present this steak on a cutting board with a carving knife.

BOURBON BBQ RIBS

T FUSION

OWNER/CHEF
*Owner Allison Kahn /
Chef Daniel Rivera*

LOCATION
*Marine
Park,
Brooklyn,
New York*

Not everyone believed that we'd be able to complete a book like this, and our publisher agreed that if we could, it would be a great accomplishment. During one visit to the ArtScroll offices after the recipes were compiled and photographed, we were asked, "Did you get T Fusion?"

Our response, "The BBQ ribs."

We saw eyes light up. We know why. This is a truly special recipe, from a veteran and accomplished chef. T Fusion's Executive Chef Daniel Rivera keeps the menu true to the restaurant's name, with interesting fusions of flavors from a variety of cuisines. Favorite appetizers also include their signature Chicken Crisps or the Charcuterie board, and entrées such as the Delmonico or Reserve Steaks aged 21-plus days. (They're not just great cuts of meat. Chef Rivera brings out their best with the right marinades and seasonings.)

Both the ambiance and the food make T Fusion a fine dining experience without leaving the neighborhood. You'll love dessert too, especially those churros served with a unique strawberry-ginger coulis dipping sauce.

Love pairing your food with wine? T Fusion has a huge selection (and a full bar that makes fun drinks) housed in a wine room filled with 375 bottles.

Regulars want to come back with lots of guests when there's an occasion to celebrate, and the large upstairs party room is always in demand. -L.

BOURBON BBQ RIBS

YIELD *6-8 servings*

CATEGORY *meat*

DESCRIPTION

Back ribs with a house spice rub and bourbon BBQ glaze

We loved this recipe so much and prepared it very, very often. Victoria didn't want to give it up even for Passover. Even though she had to leave out a few ingredients, it still came out spectacular.

INGREDIENTS

- 4   racks of ribs *(approx. 4-5 ribs per rack)*
- •   oil, *for searing*

  beef stock, *as needed*
- 4 TSP   liquid smoke

DRY SPICE RUB:

¼ CUP	chili powder
¼ CUP	coffee
3 TBSP	onion powder
1 TBSP	dried dill weed
3 TBSP	garlic powder
2 TBSP	kosher salt
2 TBSP	pepper
3 TBSP	cumin
6 TBSP	dark brown sugar
1 TBSP	dried basil
1 TBSP	oregano
1 TBSP	rosemary
1 TBSP	thyme
2 TBSP	smoked paprika
2 TBSP	coriander

BARBECUE SAUCE:

½	onion
4	garlic cloves
¾ CUP	Maker's Mark Bourbon
2½ CUPS	ketchup
⅓ CUP	apple cider vinegar
1½ TBSP	liquid smoke
½ CUP	brown sugar
½ CUP	honey
1 TSP	sriracha sauce
6 TBSP	fish-free Worcestershire sauce
•	kosher salt and pepper, *to taste*

INSTRUCTIONS

1 Preheat oven to 400°F.

2 In a medium bowl, combine all spice rub ingredients (if you are not preparing 4 racks, divide the spice rub and store the remainder for the next time this recipe is prepared).

3 Rub beef racks all over with spice rub.

4 Heat oil in a large sauté pan over medium-high heat, or preferably, preheat a grill and rub with oil. Once pan or grill is hot, add meat and sear until browned on all sides, about 4 minutes per side.

5 Fill a roasting pan (or two) halfway with beef stock. Add liquid smoke. Place meat in pan, meat side up and bones curving down. Cover tightly with foil and cook for 5 hours. (Fewer racks may cook in less time, 3-4 hours.) Check the pan frequently to make sure it has plenty of liquid; add beef stock as necessary throughout the cooking process.

6 Meanwhile, prepare the barbecue sauce: In a food processor, combine all ingredients. (If you are not preparing 4 racks, divide the barbecue sauce and store the remainder in the refrigerator for the next time this recipe is prepared.)

7 Glaze the ribs generously with the barbecue sauce and return to oven, uncovered, for 15 minutes.

Not making four racks of ribs? When you put your extra spice rub away, be sure to do it before you coat the ribs, so it doesn't come into contact with the raw meat. Because there are so many ingredients, we highly recommend making the complete spice rub and barbecue sauce even if you're serving just one or two racks. You will be making this again.

CHINESE-STYLE GLAZED CORNED BEEF

Because our food is better.™

YUSSI'S

OWNER/CHEF

*Owner Yussi Weisz /
Chef Shmuli Schwinger*

LOCATION

*Two locations in
Lakewood, New Jersey*

Leah and I scheduled a meeting with Yussi to determine which recipe we should feature in this book. But we hadn't mentioned where the meeting would take place.

"It must be the Second Street location," Leah said. "He's there whenever I go."

"But he's also always at the Westgate location when I go," I responded.

Maybe there are two Yussis?

Yussi is the king of takeout in Lakewood. The original location, Yussi's Deli, buzzes on Thursdays and Fridays, when local residents pop in for their Shabbos must-haves: six varieties of chummus, coleslaw, spicy mayo, herring, chicken with kishka, pepper-crusted roast, and the most popular meat: this Chinese-Style Corned Beef. Yussi's chef-run takeout kitchen

is led by Executive Chef Shmuli Schwinger. When I walked in, I was amazed at the variety. My first thought was, "When you live around here, why cook?"

Yussi's Grill, at the other end of town, is a family-friendly sit-down restaurant, with a grill, deli, and a sushi menu (worth a trip if you're a sushi-lover!). Favorites include what regulars call the "Heart Attack Sandwich" (grilled kishka, pastrami, and sautéed fresh mushrooms and onions), the Creamy Garlic Steak Sandwich, the Pastrami Burger, and Chicken Caesar Salad. On the sushi menu, we love Kani Poppers, Kani Salad, and tempura-style rolls like Hillside Run.

The bottom line: When I'm in Lakewood, this is where I go when I want to feed my family reliably good food. It helps that the fries are awesome. - V.

CHINESE-STYLE GLAZED CORNED BEEF

YIELD *8-10 servings*

CATEGORY *meat*

DESCRIPTION

Corned beef with a sweet and salty Asian glaze

Construction for the first Yussi's location began on September 11, 2001. The deli and takeout opened the following January. Yussi was only 21 years old at the time. As a yeshivah boy, he had been known for making and selling a good cholent.

INGREDIENTS

4-5 LB	first cut pickled corned beef
1 CUP	low sodium soy sauce
1 CUP	duck sauce
2 TBSP	chopped garlic
1¼ CUPS	brown sugar
¼ CUP	teriyaki sauce
¼ TSP	red #40 *(food coloring)*, *optional*

INSTRUCTIONS

1 Add corned beef to a large pot. Cover generously with water. Bring water to a boil over high heat and let cook for 2 hours. Remove from heat and let corned beef cool in the water. At this point, the pot can be covered and left to cool in the refrigerator overnight if desired.

2 In a medium bowl or jar, combine soy sauce, duck sauce, garlic, brown sugar, teriyaki sauce, and red #40 (optional).

3 Preheat oven to 375°F.

4 Place corned beef on a baking sheet. Cover very well with sauce. Bake for 30 minutes, or until edges crisp up. Let cool before slicing.

When you look at the showcase, you'll admit it: that deep mahogany sauce looks really appealing. Psychologically, red is the number one most attention-grabbing color, which is why it's added to many dishes. In nature, red fruit denotes ripeness. The pinker salmon and the redder tuna denote quality. And while you only need a bit to give this sauce that vibrant look, the red coloring only affects the color and the sales appeal, not the taste.

In the Yussi's showcase are perfectly cooked pieces of roast, with just the right amount of pink in the middle. So we asked Chef Schwinger, "How can you tell when a roast is done?" He told us:

"Don't be afraid to rely on a meat thermometer. We'll cook a roast to 140°F for perfect doneness, but that doesn't mean you leave it in until it reaches that. If you take it out at 120°F and tent it with foil, the internal temperature will continue to rise."

- CHEF SHMULI SCHWINGER, YUSSI'S

SLOW-COOKED OKINAWA RIBS

INGREDIENTS

2 TSP	canola or vegetable oil
2½-3 LB	beef or veal spare ribs, *cut into 2-2 ½-inch pieces*
3½ OZ	fresh ginger, *peeled and cut into thick slices*
2 CUPS	low-sodium chicken or beef broth
⅓ CUP	packed dark brown sugar
¼ CUP	mirin
⅔ CUP	sake
½ CUP	shoyu sauce *(Japanese soy sauce)*

YIELD *4-6 servings*

CATEGORY *meat*

DESCRIPTION

Braised spare ribs in a sweet and savory Asian-style sauce

Sometimes you find gems in the most unexpected places — like Phoenix. And sometimes, after testing two recipes from one restaurant, we couldn't choose between them. These outrageous ribs are from **SEGAL'S**, *the restaurant that gave us Eggplant Chicken in Garlic Sauce on page 124.*

INSTRUCTIONS

1. Heat oil in heavy saucepan over high heat. Add ribs and brown meat on all sides.

2. Rinse meat; remove and discard excess fat from pan. Return meat to pan; add cold water to cover well.

3. Add ginger; bring to boil over high heat. Reduce heat and simmer for 2 hours.

4. Discard liquid and ginger. Set meat aside.

5. Place broth, brown sugar, mirin, sake, and shoyu into a clean, heavy saucepan. Stir over high heat until sugar has dissolved.

6. Add meat and bring to boil. Reduce heat and let simmer for 1 hour, turning occasionally.

7. Remove from heat. Let meat rest in liquid for 20 minutes. Remove meat to a platter or bowl; cover with foil to keep warm.

8. Return saucepan to high heat; bring liquid to a boil. Cook until sauce is slightly syrupy. Return meat to sauce and coat well.

BOLOGNESE

BISTRO NATALIE

OWNER/CHEF
Chef Todd Aarons

LOCATION
Los Angeles, California

We didn't aim to feature any new restaurants in this book, but rather those that have already proven themselves with time. But when I heard that the owners had tapped the talent of Executive Chef Todd Aarons to take the helm of Bistro Natalie, Pico Boulevard's newest jewel, that was enough to immediately catapult Bistro Natalie, with its Mediterranean-inspired French cuisine, into a class of its own.

Chef Todd's resume reads like a novel, from the world-class chefs who were his mentors, to his inspired years in Tuscany and then Jerusalem, where kosher became his new inspiration. He became renowned for his work at Tierra Sur at the Herzog Winery (see page 266), where he reinvented fine kosher dining by bringing all of his experiences together to create a rustic cuisine inspired by his international travels and the seasonal produce from the area's farmers.

This is why we're excited about Bistro Natalie. At the restaurant, the breads, pastas, and charcuterie are made from scratch. Though the menu isn't large, it is expertly crafted, and the unique food pairings are evidence that there's a master chef in the back of the house. Diners have been wowed from the beginning of the meal with the Salade Maison (with fried chickpeas), the Chorizo & Egg (frisee salad with lardons, pickled onions, and a roasted tomato vinaigrette), and Empanadas filled with lamb birria and sweet potato with a chimichurri dipping sauce. The steaks are perfectly cooked in a wood-fired oven, the salmon is smoked in cherry wood, and the lamb is served with pickled eggplant and chickpea fries; they all come together to bring diners the perfect marriage of flavor and technique. -V.

OSSO BUCO

THE HARBOUR GRILL

OWNER/CHEF
Owner Gilbert Amsellem/
Chef David Benrey

LOCATION
Surfside,
Florida

When we say "Surfside," you might not be familiar with which Miami-Dade County neighborhood we're referring to, but if we said instead "right next to Bal Harbour," you'd immediately agree that it's the perfect spot for an elegant night out.

In some towns, it's easy to find a great place to eat an amazing kosher meal. Just walk down one street and take your pick. There's Pico Boulevard in Los Angeles, Central Avenue in the Five Towns, and then there's Harding Avenue in Miami, where Harbour Grill is located, two blocks south of the Bal Harbour Shops. Harding Avenue has become the Surfside block synonymous with fine kosher dining (for dairy on Harding, see page 230). Lots of New Yorkers look forward to their Florida vacations when they can return to Surfside to enjoy unique sushi (which looks like art on a plate and includes options like a sea bass roll or coconut "shrimp" tempura), along with Kobe Wagyu beef burgers and aged steaks (including the King Reserve, the Outlaw, and the Steak Teriyaki). Popular specials on the menu include this Osso Buco, prepared in the traditional style. Just don't forget to make reservations, especially in the winter months. - L.

OSSO BUCO

YIELD *8 servings*

CATEGORY *meat*

DESCRIPTION

Veal shanks braised in an herbed red wine tomato sauce; served with gremolata

Osso Buco is a great dish for Friday nights and holiday meals, when you need a dish that can be prepared ahead.

INGREDIENTS

½ CUP	olive oil
2 TBSP	margarine
8	veal shanks *(osso buco)*
•	kosher salt
•	black pepper
½ CUP	flour
6	garlic cloves, *minced*
2 CUPS	chopped onions
2 CUPS	chopped carrots
2 CUPS	chopped celery
12 OZ	tomato paste
4 CUPS	dry red wine
8 CUPS	beef stock

BOUQUET GARNI:

2	sprigs fresh thyme
2	bay leaves
2	sprigs fresh rosemary

GREMOLATA:

¼ CUP	finely chopped fresh parsley
•	zest of 1 lemon
3	garlic cloves, *minced*

INSTRUCTIONS

1 Preheat oven to 350°F.

2 Heat oil with margarine in a large Dutch oven over medium heat.

3 Season veal shanks with salt and pepper; dust with flour. Add veal shanks to pan and lightly brown on all sides. Remove veal shanks from pan. Add garlic, onions, carrots, and celery; sauté for 5-7 minutes. While sautéing, scrape up the brown bits from the bottom of the pan.

4 Lower heat, add tomato paste, and cook for 5 minutes, stirring constantly. Add red wine and cook for 3 minutes. Add beef stock.

5 Prepare the bouquet garni: Tie together the thyme, bay leaves, and rosemary with kitchen twine (or add to bouquet garni bag) and add to pan.

6 Return shanks to the pan. Season with salt and pepper. Cover; bake 1½ hours, until meat is tender. If sauce is too thin, remove shanks and reduce sauce on the stove until desired thickness is reached.

7 Prepare the gremolata: In a small bowl, combine parsley, lemon zest, and garlic.

8 To serve, pour sauce over shanks and top with gremolata. Serve over mashed potatoes or rice.

CLOSER LOOK *Gremolata, an herb-based condiment, is the traditional accompaniment to Osso Buco. Although this version, made with lemon zest, parsley, and garlic, is the classic version, variations can include different herbs and/or the zest of different citrus fruits.*

TIDBIT *Harbour Grill's owner, Gilbert Amsellem, learned to make sushi during his travels to Asia. Back in the U.S., his impressed guests urged him to do something with his talent. After he acquired The Harbour Grill, the rest is history. Food is definitely the owner's true passion and life calling.*

CLOSER LOOK *A bouquet garni is a bundle of herbs. They're used to flavor stocks and sauces, and are bundled together to make them easy to remove once their job is done.*

MONGOLIAN BEEF

TK ASIAN FUSION

OWNER/CHEF
Owner Eddie Hakim

LOCATION
Oakhurst, New Jersey

TK Asian Fusion is upscale Asian — while you'll get great versions of the classic Chinese and Japanese dishes, you'll remember your meal best after you've sat in the back around the hibachi. A hibachi is a heated cooking surface, and tables and chairs surround it in a U-shape.

We ordered from the hibachi menu, and the chef came to the table with the raw ingredients. Once the hibachi was hot, it was time for the show. There were definitely some acrobatics and knife juggling, but then the theatrics got more intense. Our chef drew a smiley face on the hibachi using oil, then lit the smiley on fire. Then came my favorite hibachi moment: After swiftly slicing some onions into thick rings, our chef stacked the onions, with the largest rings on the bottom and smallest on top, forming a volcano-shaped mound. Squirt some oil into the volcano, light it up, and presto: an erupting volcano, the highlight of the show.

Finally, it was time to actually cook the food, which took just moments, due to the heat of the surface. As the chef finished each component (steak, chicken, veggies, and noodles), he placed it on the plate. Of course, I asked him what was in each squirt bottle he used to flavor the food.

Aside from the entertainment, TK Asian Fusion has an extensive Asian menu, including some unique options, such as Spicy Tuna "Meatballs," which are rolled in tempura flakes and fried; Pad Thai in a tamarind sauce; and Fish Tacos, which include fried tilapia, apple, and Asian pears. In addition to the fun (both on the menu and in the dining room), the dish we keep hearing we have to try at TK Asian Fusion is the Mongolian Beef. -V.

MONGOLIAN BEEF

YIELD *1 serving*

CATEGORY *meat*

DESCRIPTION
Tender marinated shredded beef sautéed with ginger, scallion, onion, red and green peppers in a special seasoned miso sauce

Cornstarch and egg white are used to soften chicken or beef in Asian dishes. This process is called velveting. This marinade can coat up to 1½ pounds of meat if you're making multiple batches.

INGREDIENTS

½ LB	beef *(see note on facing page), thinly sliced*
•	kosher salt
•	pepper
1	egg white
1 TBSP	cornstarch
•	oil, *for frying*
1	onion, *cut into thin strips*
1	long hot pepper, *cut into rings*
2	scallions, *cut into 3-inch pieces*
2 TBSP	sugar
2 TBSP	hoisin sauce
2 TBSP	soy sauce
2 TSP	sesame oil

INSTRUCTIONS

1. In a small bowl, combine beef, salt, pepper, and egg white. Mix in cornstarch. Marinate overnight (see note on facing page).

2. Heat wok over high heat. When pan is hot, add oil for deep-frying. Add beef and deep-fry until cooked, 3-4 minutes. Set aside. Pour oil from pan, leaving just 1-2 tablespoons.

3. Add onion and pepper to wok. Stir-fry for 1-2 minutes. Add scallions and beef. Add in sugar, hoisin sauce, soy sauce, and sesame oil; cook briefly while stirring until meat and vegetables are coated. Serve immediately.

CLOSER LOOK *Hoisin sauce is the barbecue sauce of Chinese cuisine that's thick in consistency. Though it contains soy, it has a greater depth of flavor, due to the rice vinegar, garlic, and seasonings. Its flavor is salty and sweet and very intense — you only need a little bit in a dish.*

To get this recipe perfect, we went behind the scenes and watched TK Asian Fusion's chef in action. At Asian restaurants like this one, dishes are prepared in single portions in a wok set over an open fire pit. Preheat your pan until very hot to get the same results at home.

Neck meat, silvertip, or rib eye will work well in this recipe.

SALMON & TUNA WITH TERIYAKI SAUCE

RIMŌN||מון
RESTAURANT · CAFÉ

CAFÉ RIMON

OWNER/CHEF
Chef Erez Ben Uria

LOCATION

Two Jerusalem, Israel locations; off Ben Yehudah Street and in the Mamilla Mall

There's something unique about Café Rimon in the Mamilla Mall that makes me really enjoy the Jerusalem afternoons I spent there, aside from the gorgeous views overlooking the walls of the Old City (for more on the Rimon family of restaurants, see page 90). Because of its location in Jerusalem's most upscale shopping district, the restaurant draws an eclectic international crowd. Above the din of forks and knives, you can hear conversations in a dozen different languages.

I suppose that means the Café Rimon strikes a chord with a huge variety of people and taste buds.

Café Rimon favorites include the Hot Camembert Sandwich … Belgian Waffles topped with ice cream, caramel, and white chocolate … Cauliflower with Techineh … Hot Asian Vegetable and Noodle Stir-Fry (with ginger soy sauce, date honey, and haloumi cheese) … and these really good and intensely flavorful salmon and tuna fingers. -L.

SALMON & TUNA WITH TERIYAKI SAUCE

YIELD *4 servings*

CATEGORY *pareve*

DESCRIPTION
Pan-seared salmon and tuna, served with our special teriyaki sauce, onions, mushrooms, scallions, and cashews

This Teriyaki Sauce will make a double recipe, but since it takes some time to make, it's worthwhile to save the rest of the sauce for the next time you enjoy this dish, or for any recipe that calls for teriyaki sauce.

INGREDIENTS

3-4 TBSP	olive oil, *divided*
2	red onions, *thinly sliced*
1 LB	mushrooms, *quartered*
1 LB	salmon, *skin removed, cut into 1-in wide strips*
1 LB	tuna, *cut into 1-in wide strips*
•	kosher salt, *to taste*
•	pinch coarse black pepper
2	scallions, *green parts only, cut into rings*
½ CUP	cashews
⅓ CUP	sesame seeds

TERIYAKI SAUCE:

1 CUP	sugar
2	carrots, *finely diced*
1	onion, *diced*
1	celery rib, *diced*
2 OZ	fresh ginger root, *peeled and sliced*
4	garlic cloves, *minced*
½ CUP	white wine
2 CUPS	low-sodium soy sauce
3 TBSP	cornstarch dissolved in 5 Tbsp water
•	lettuce, *for plating*

INSTRUCTIONS

1 Prepare the teriyaki sauce: Add sugar to a medium saucepan over medium-low heat; caramelize sugar. When the sugar at the edges of the pan begins to melt, gently stir. Continue to stir gently until sugar is liquefied. (If your sugar turns into rocks, it's too cold. Raise heat and let it warm up, then gently stir.)

2 Add carrots, onion, celery, ginger, and garlic and cook over medium-low heat, stirring constantly, for 5 minutes. Some of the sugar may harden; that's okay. Add white wine and cook an additional 5 minutes.

3 Add soy sauce and bring to a simmer. Lower heat; simmer for 1 hour.

4 Strain out vegetables and return sauce to the pan. Bring to a boil over high heat. Stir in cornstarch mixture. When sauce reaches desired consistency, remove from heat. Set aside.

5 Prepare the fish: Heat 1 table-spoon olive oil in a large sauté pan over medium heat. Add onions; cook until soft, about 5 minutes. Add mushrooms and cook until completely soft and tender, about 20-30 minutes. Remove from pan and set aside.

6 In the same pan, heat remaining olive oil. Once oil is hot, add fish. Sear on all sides until medium-rare (the tuna will cook much faster than the salmon; remove while you still see pink inside). Remove from pan and set aside.

7 Return vegetables to the pan. Stir in ¾ cup teriyaki sauce and cook for 1 minute. Taste and season with salt and pepper if necessary (extra salt may not be necessary, depending on the type of soy sauce used).

8 Spread lettuce onto each plate. Arrange salmon and tuna in a row on top. Top with mushroom/teriyaki mixture and sprinkle with scallions, cashews, and sesame seeds. Drizzle 1-2 additional tablespoons teriyaki sauce on top.

CLOSER LOOK

While we usually use fresh ginger in its minced form, since here it's just used to infuse flavor into the sauce, it's fine to simply slice it up. If you keep cubes of frozen ginger in your freezer, those will work too. A few cubes will do the job.

Prefer salmon over tuna or vice versa? Choose your favorite.

For more on caramelizing sugar, see page 13 in Techniques.

TILAPIA WITH TERRA CHIP CRUNCH

THE PURPLE PEAR

OWNER/CHEF
Owner Jack Kotlar

LOCATION
Monsey, New York

The Purple Pear is perhaps Monsey's favorite restaurant, and rumor had it that the recipes are very safely guarded. The Purple Pear was opened in the summer of 2006 by Jack Kotlar and Malki Levine, who developed the recipes. Most of the items on the menu, including this tilapia, are original favorites.

The Purple Pear is a casual café-style restaurant that's a great spot to meet friends or family for lunch or a dairy dinner. There's a large, fun menu (filled with lots of salads, sandwiches, wraps, pasta, and fish dishes) that includes both kid-friendly dishes (one section of the menu is called "fun stuff" and includes dishes such as Pizza Pockets and Sweet Potato Fries with a cinnamon-sugar dip) and dishes that appeal to more sophisticated taste buds, such as the Sesame Salmon Salad with Edamame and Ginger Dressing and the Portobello Mushroom Ravioli. **- L.**

One of the biggest revelations while working on this book came while I was mixing the marinade for this recipe for the first time. As I added all these spices into the mixture, I thought, "I never, in a million years, would have thought of a recipe like this." That's what's so special about this book — learning new culinary perspectives. Even if I never could have imagined developing this recipe on my own, it's become one of my family's favorite fish dishes. **- V.**

TILAPIA WITH TERRA CHIP CRUNCH

YIELD *4 servings*

CATEGORY *pareve*

DESCRIPTION
Tilapia marinated in a sweet and savory dressing and topped with Sun-Dried Tomato Terra Chip crunch

The most frequently asked question at The Purple Pear is, "Why are your walls red if your name is The Purple Pear?"

INGREDIENTS

2 LB	tilapia fillets
1	bag Terra Sticks, *crushed to a coarse crumb*
1	bag Sun Dried Tomato Terra Chips, *crushed to a coarse crumb*

MARINADE:

½ CUP	light corn syrup
¼ CUP	yellow mustard
¼ CUP	red wine vinegar
•	pinch turmeric
¾ TSP	thyme
¾ TSP	rosemary
4 TSP	garlic powder
4 TSP	granulated garlic
4 TSP	onion powder
4 TSP	granulated onion
1 TBSP	paprika
½ TSP	coarse black pepper
1 TBSP	brown sugar
2-3 TBSP	lemon juice
•	pinch kosher salt
3 TBSP	soybean oil

INSTRUCTIONS

1 In a medium bowl, combine all marinade ingredients. At The Purple Pear, this is done using an immersion blender. Add fish and marinate for 1 hour.

2 Preheat oven to 350°F. Line a baking sheet with parchment paper.

3 Remove fish from marinade; discard marinade. Place fish on prepared baking sheet. Cover top of fish well with crumbs. Bake for 17 minutes.

CLOSER LOOK *What's the difference between granulated garlic or onion and garlic or onion powder? Just the texture. If you don't have both, simply double up on the one you have.*

We love using sole or flounder in this recipe instead of tilapia.

If you can't find these varieties of Terra Chips, most flavors that the brand produces will work nicely. Though you can crush the chips (as shown) in a plastic bag, for a prettier crust, pulse the chips in the food processor.

BLACKENED FISH

FISH GRILL

OWNER/CHEF
Owner Aharon Klein

LOCATION
*Five locations in
Los Angeles, California*

Through this past year, we asked everyone we met about their favorite restaurants. Anyone who lives in or has ever been to L.A. kept talking fondly about Fish Grill. But whenever we asked which recipe they liked there, they'd tell us, "You can't copy their food with a recipe. The restaurant is great because the fish is super fresh and it's cooked on a mesquite grill."

The mesquite wood used to cook the fish at Fish Grill adds a unique flavor that can't be attained using other cooking methods. It also burns hotter and longer than other woods — cooking fish quickly at those high temperatures keeps it juicy and preserves the flavor.

The first Fish Grill, on Beverly Boulevard in Los Angeles, opened in 1986 after owner Aharon Klein took his passion for grilling and fresh fish beyond that backyard barbecue. The restaurants are super-casual spots, the prices are affordable, and many appreciate that they can actually enjoy a meal that's healthy.

What do diners absolutely love? We keep hearing about the Fish Tacos (see Tidbit on page 205). The Salmon Pasta (made with grilled salmon and angel hair pasta) and Fish and Chips are also favorites.

If you don't want your fish grilled, it can also be ordered blackened. Blackening fish creates a crisp, spicy crust, sealing in the juices. And since it's done in a skillet, it's something we can do too to enjoy Fish Grill's taste of the sea. - V.

BLACKENED FISH

YIELD 4-6 servings

CATEGORY
pareve or dairy

DESCRIPTION
Cajun-spiced fish, cooked quickly in a cast-iron skillet, with a crisp exterior and moist interior

Blackening means to cook (usually fish) on a high temperature for a short period of time, until the spices form a black crust. The key to successful blackening is that super-hot pan. The most common type of blackened fish uses Cajun seasoning.

INGREDIENTS

2½ TSP	kosher salt
¾ TSP	freshly ground black pepper
¾ TSP	ground white pepper
1 TSP	cayenne pepper
1 TSP	garlic powder
1 TSP	onion powder
½ TSP	thyme
½ TSP	oregano
1 TBSP	sweet paprika
10 TBSP	vegetable oil, *divided (OR melted butter if desired)*
4-6	*(½-in-thick)* 8-oz fillets of skinless and boneless tilapia or red snapper, *or other mild-tasting white fish*
•	lemon wedges OR melted butter, *for serving*

INSTRUCTIONS

1. Open windows or use over-the-stove exhaust fan, as this cooking method will produce smoke.

2. In a wide dish, combine salt, black pepper, white pepper, cayenne pepper, garlic powder, onion powder, thyme, oregano, and paprika. Set aside.

3. Pour oil or butter into a bowl and coat each fillet well (reserve the remaining oil for step 4). Generously sprinkle the spice mixture on each fillet; rub into the fish.

4. Heat a heavy skillet (cast iron is best) over high heat for about 5 minutes or until it begins to smoke and bottom of pan lightens in color. Add 2-3 fillets to the hot pan. Pour about 1 teaspoon of oil or melted butter over each fillet. Cook over high heat about 1½ minutes. Turn fish over and pour another teaspoon of oil or melted butter over fish. Cook another 1½ minutes or until the fillets are blackened. Repeat process with remaining fillets. Serve immediately with wedges of lemon or melted butter, if desired.

CLOSER LOOK *All these spices combined are considered "Cajun spice." This mixture will also work well on your French fries (as recommended on page 10) or sprinkled on your eye of the rib fillet (on page 164). Be aware: it's spicy! For a milder version, go lighter on the cayenne.*

A cast-iron skillet is the secret weapon for many chefs, and it's an inexpensive investment for the home cook too. Your cast-iron skillet will last forever, and can withstand much higher temperatures than your standard cookware. And because it can get so hot, food cooked in cast iron will have many similar properties to food cooked on a grill (including that nice crust). One caveat: Cast iron cannot go in the dishwasher.

TIDBIT *Fish Grill is famous for its own Fish Tacos, with salsa, cabbage, and its special sauce inside a corn tortilla. Make this recipe into a complete dinner at home by making your own tacos. We loved strips of this fish inside wraps or tortillas, topped with a slaw, corn or tomato salsa, and an avocado-mayo sauce.*

SALMON WITH LEMON & CAPER SAUCE

BEYOND BY SHEMTOV'S

OWNER/CHEF
Owner Baruch Sandhaus

LOCATION
On 41st Street in Miami Beach, Florida

Since 2005, Shemtov's has been the star of 41st Street in Miami Beach. Owner Baruch Sandhaus, though, had a different vision for the popular pizzeria … he wanted to "wow" diners and give them an experience that goes beyond the standard pizzeria lunch … hence the name "Beyond by Shemtov's" (for more on restaurateur Baruch Sandhaus's restaurants, see page 102).

Today, Beyond by Shemtov's is a hip restaurant serving every meal of the day in a modern, fun, and casual atmosphere. Get your smoothie, freshly squeezed orange juice, or iced coffee while on the go in the morning; get a Miami Heat pizza and milkshake for lunch; come for a fish or pasta dinner (and enjoy options like Teriyaki Salmon Sliders with wasabi mayo or a Five-Cheese Lasagna) … or just stop by for some froyo or a dessert crepe (like the one loaded with caramelized bananas, whipped cream, cinnamon, and dulce de leche).

Because the selection is so vast, with anything you could possibly be in the mood to eat, the menu appeals to all those enjoying the Miami sun: Miami residents and their kids, tourists, and Miami seniors (it's probably both the grandchild's and grandmother's favorite lunch spot). During the winter season, it's packed during lunchtime and shortly after for dinner, when dishes like this salmon are popular. - L.

SALMON WITH LEMON & CAPER SAUCE

YIELD *4 servings*

CATEGORY *dairy*

DESCRIPTION
Pan-seared salmon with a shallot and lemon sauce highlighted with capers and fresh parsley

You'll get about 3 tablespoons of juice from the average-sized lemon. Bring your lemons to room temperature or warm them briefly in the microwave for easier squeezing.

INGREDIENTS

4	*(6-oz)* salmon fillets
•	kosher salt, *for sprinkling*
•	coarse black pepper, *for sprinkling*
1½ Tbsp	unsalted butter
1½ Tbsp	olive oil
1	garlic clove, *minced*
2	shallots, *minced*
⅔ cup	white wine
3 Tbsp	fresh lemon juice
3 Tbsp	small capers
1 Tbsp	fresh parsley, *chopped*

CLOSER LOOK *Capers are tiny round fleshy buds that are sold in their pickled form in little glass jars. In your supermarket, they'll either be located near the pickles and olives, or on the shelf near other Italian ingredients (like the canned or sun-dried tomatoes). And though they may be tiny, don't skip them. They pack big flavor.*

INSTRUCTIONS

1. Season salmon fillets lightly with salt and pepper.

2. Melt butter with olive oil in a large frying pan over medium heat.

3. Add fillets to the pan and cook, turning once, until seared brown on both sides, about 6-8 minutes total. Transfer fillets to a warm plate and cover with foil.

4. Add garlic and shallots to the pan and cook, stirring frequently, until the shallots are just opaque, 1-2 minutes. Add white wine; reduce for 2 minutes. Add lemon juice. Increase heat to medium-high; bring to a boil. Let boil until sauce thickens slightly. (Optional: For a smooth sauce, as shown, transfer sauce to a blender. Blend until smooth and return to the pan.)

5. Stir in capers and parsley. To serve, pour sauce over salmon fillets or plate the salmon over the sauce.

RARE BISTRO'S "CRAB" CAKES

One of Beyond by Shemtov's sister restaurants, Rare Bistro, is just a couple blocks away, serving inventive yet casual fare. For more on the Rare Group's family of restaurants, see page 102.

YIELD *12 small "crab" cakes*

1 LB	kani *(imitation crab)*
2 TBSP	oil
1 CUP	finely diced red pepper
1 CUP	finely diced green pepper
1 CUP	finely diced red onion
3	eggs, *divided*
¼ CUP	chopped cilantro
¼ CUP	chopped scallion
¾ CUP	mayonnaise
½ TBSP	Dijon mustard
½ CUP	grated white horseradish
2 TSP	Old Bay seasoning
1 TSP	cayenne pepper
½ CUP	panko crumbs, *plus more for breading*
1 TSP	salt
•	pinch coarse black pepper
•	flour, *for breading*
•	vegetable oil, *for deep frying*

1. In a food processor, pulse the kani until it is finely chopped. It is important to use the pulse button so it does not become a paste, which will be difficult to work with.

2. Heat oil in a sauté pan over medium heat. Add peppers and onion; sauté until soft, about 10 minutes. In a large bowl, combine sautéed vegetables, kani, 1 egg, cilantro, scallion, mayonnaise, mustard, horseradish, Old Bay seasoning, cayenne pepper, and ½ cup panko crumbs. If the mixture is too crumbly, add more panko crumbs. Season with salt and pepper. Shape mixture into patties.

3. Prepare three bowls. Place flour into one; 2 eggs, beaten, in the second; and panko crumbs in the third. Coat the patties with flour, dip in the egg, and coat with panko.

4. Heat oil in a deep fryer or saucepan to between 350ºF and 375ºF. Add patties; fry until golden. Serve with tartar sauce or Old Bay aioli (fresh mayonnaise including Old Bay seasoning).

MISO-TOMATO SEA BASS

DAY FiVE

DAY FIVE

OWNER/CHEF
Owner Raizy Levine / Chef Nima Sherpa

LOCATION

NEW YORK CITY

The Midwood neighborhood of Brooklyn, New York

In the kosher world today, there are lots of cafés and steakhouses that also serve sushi. Day Five, though, is completely dedicated to the art: It's an authentic kosher Japanese restaurant. The chef trained with the world's elite sushi masters and came to Day Five after heading some of the most illustrious non-kosher sushi restaurants.

At Day Five, the menu is exciting, vibrant, and healthful (unless you indulge in the tempura). All the fish is fresh from the market every morning … and lots of that fish make it onto Day Five's Tuna Pizza (thin slices of raw tuna on crispy dough, topped with veggies, sauce, and sprouts), the restaurant's most popular dish.

Other starters include Spicy Kani Salad, Yellowtail Jalapeños, and Sweetheart and Fireman rolls. (Like your sushi spicy?)

The soups are nourishing and pack flavor in every spoonful. Even the side dishes, like the string beans, round out the Day Five experience: they're pan-seared in a garlic-miso sauce.

"I've been eating something different from the menu every single day and I'm still not bored," says owner Raizy Levine. She enjoys the full gamut of the variety, including the naruto — carb-free sushi without seaweed or rice. Rather, it's wrapped in cucumber and filled with components that include marinated daikon.

Don't know what to pick? Get a Bento Box for lunch and enjoy a little bit of everything. Or come back for dinner and enjoy one of the elegantly plated fresh fish entrees, like this one. - V.

MISO-TOMATO SEA BASS

YIELD *4 servings*

CATEGORY
dairy/pareve

Day Five is named after the fifth day of creation, when fish were created.

DESCRIPTION

Sea bass served over a sushi rice cake with a side of zucchini noodles

INGREDIENTS

SEA BASS:

4	*(3-oz)* sea bass fillets, *with skin*
•	kosher salt
•	coarse black pepper
2 TSP	oil OR nonstick cooking spray, *for coating pan*

MISO-TOMATO SAUCE:

2	garlic cloves
1 TBSP	sugar
½ TBSP	white miso paste
½ TBSP	sesame seeds
½ TBSP	kosher salt
1 CUP	extra virgin olive oil
1	*(28-oz)* can whole peeled tomatoes, *with its liquid*

ZUCCHINI NOODLES:

1 TSP	butter *(or margarine)*
3 MEDIUM	zucchini
1 CUP	Miso-Tomato Sauce, *above*
½ TSP	soy sauce

CRISPY RICE CAKE:

1⅓ CUPS	cooked sushi rice, *mixed with 2 Tbsp rice vinegar, 1 Tbsp sugar, and ½ tsp salt*
4 TBSP	sesame seeds
•	flour, *for dredging*
•	oil, *for frying*

INSTRUCTIONS

1 Prepare the sauce: In the jar of a blender, combine garlic, sugar, miso paste, sesame seeds, salt, olive oil, and tomatoes. (This sauce is best when prepared 1-2 days in advance, allowing time for the ingredients to meld and develop richer flavor).

2 Prepare the zucchini noodles: Using a vegetable peeler, slice zucchini into long strips. Heat butter and 1 cup Miso-Tomato Sauce in a sauté pan over medium-high heat. Stir in soy sauce. Add zucchini noodles and cook, stirring often, until noodles absorb the sauce and soften, about 6 minutes.

3 Prepare the crispy rice cake: Combine rice and sesame seeds. Press ⅓ cup rice-sesame mixture into the bottom of a (4-inch) round container to form a disc. Remove and dredge in flour. Repeat with remaining rice.

4 Heat oil in a deep fryer or sauté pan with at least 1-inch oil. When oil is hot, add rice cake and fry for 3 minutes on the first side, and 2 minutes on the second side, or until golden brown.

5 Season sea bass with salt and pepper.

6 Heat a skillet over high heat. Add oil; place sea bass, skin side down, and cook for 3 minutes. Flip and cook an additional 2-3 minutes or until cooked through.

7 To plate, place a rice cake on the dish. Top with sea bass. Serve zucchini noodles on the top of the sea bass or on the side. Drizzle fish with additional sauce. Serve immediately.

TIDBIT *The chef didn't really like it when Raizy wanted to put French fries on the menu, but he had to agree. After all, even in an authentic sushi and fish restaurant, you need to please the crowds.*

Yes, you can make the rice cakes featured in this recipe in advance. In fact, they'll be even crispier after they are frozen. If making in advance, fry for 1-2 additional minutes.

DINNER PARTY / SHEVA BERACHOT

MEAT

STARTER

House Salad
(page 94)

OR

Guacamole and Chips
(page 22)

OR

Duck Spring Rolls
(page 32)

MAIN

Braised Short Ribs with
Mashed Potatoes and Onions
(page 156)

DESSERT

Napoleon
(page 254)

DAIRY

STARTER

Sea Bass Spring Rolls
(page 29)

OR

Mushroom Drops
(page 18)

OR

Basil Fries
(page 48)

MAIN

Cannelloni
(page 220)

OR

Tortelloni with Sweet
Potato Ricotta Filling
(page 216)

OR

Tilapia with
Terra Chip Crunch
(page 198)

DESSERT

Chocolate Souffle
(page 270)

SERVED NEXT TO
A SCOOP OF

Cereal Milk Ice Cream
(page 276)

DAIRY

" THREE THINGS ARE GOOD IN A LITTLE
MEASURE AND BAD IN LARGE:
YEAST, SALT, AND HESITATION. "

~Talmud, Berachot 34a

TORTELLONI

CAFE · DAIRY DINING

OTTIMO CAFÉ

OWNER/CHEF

*Owner Akiva Reiner /
Chef Jason Cappetta*

LOCATION

*Right near
Lakewood
in Howell,
New Jersey*

NEW JERSEY

Ottimo Café was the first upscale dairy restaurant to open in the Lakewood area … but that doesn't mean you can't also enjoy a casual lunch there with friends. Relax in the afternoon over a salad and hot baguette, then return in the evening, when the white tablecloths are spread and the Ottimo experience is an elegant evening out when you'll enjoy food that's consistently impressive.

Owner Akiva Reiner and Chef Jason Cappetta are both committed to keeping the menu fresh and updated and the quality of each dish superb. There'll always be new, seasonal dishes to try (which is perfect since Ottimo has many customers who return on a weekly basis).

Chef Jason, a graduate of Johnson & Wales University (renowned for its top culinary program), makes the pasta from scratch.

For most pasta dishes, such as the Roasted Pepper Pappardelle, even the pasta dough itself is infused with flavors. That dish, along with this Sweet Potato Tortelloni and the Penne Jason, might be three of the best pasta dishes you've ever tried. We also love their homemade French fries with spicy aioli and the fresh Mushroom Basket with Crispy Fried Mozzarella Cheese. Their House Salad, with roasted beets, crumbled goat cheese, and a strawberry vinaigrette, makes it to almost every table, and the Potato-Crusted Salmon and Ottimo Cheese Burgers (made with fresh tuna) are two uber-popular fish dishes.

Ottimo, with its wave walls and huge party room, is also the perfect place to throw a party. Just make sure you complete the meal with one of the house-made desserts. - L.

TORTELLONI

YIELD

48 tortelloni; sauce recipe yields enough for two servings of 6 tortelloni each

CATEGORY *dairy*

DESCRIPTION

House-made pasta stuffed with sweet potato and ricotta, in an orange-brandy cream sauce

While there's nothing like fresh pasta, for a home cook shortcut we use frozen ravioli dough rounds.

INGREDIENTS

FILLING:

1½ LB	sweet potatoes, *peeled and cubed*
½ LB	ricotta cheese
½ TSP	kosher salt, *or to taste*
•	pinch coarse black pepper, *or to taste*

ASSEMBLY:

48	pasta dough circles
1	egg, *beaten*

SAUCE:

¼ CUP	*(½ stick)* unsalted butter
4 OZ	red onion, *frenched*
¼ CUP	brandy or orange liqueur
1 CUP	heavy cream
•	juice of 1 whole orange *(about ⅓ cup)*
½ TSP	kosher salt, *or to taste*
•	pinch coarse black pepper
2 TBSP	grated Parmesan cheese

INSTRUCTIONS

1. Prepare the filling: Cook sweet potatoes in a large pot of boiling water until soft. Drain sweet potatoes; purée in a food processor or mash well. Set aside to cool completely.

2. Fold ricotta into cold potatoes; season with salt and pepper. Set aside.

3. Assemble the tortelloni: On a board or flat surface, lay out the pasta dough circles (if using fresh pasta dough, you will need to flour the surface). Brush the edges with egg wash. Place a teaspoon of filling in the center of the circle. From the bottom of the circle, fold upward and seal into a half moon. Take one corner and fold it over and behind the other corner. Press firmly to seal. Freeze until ready to cook.

4. Prepare the sauce: Melt butter in a saucepan over medium heat. Add red onions and cook until golden and caramelized, about 10 minutes. Add brandy (be careful, as it may flame). Simmer for 2 minutes. Add cream and orange juice. Cook until sauce coats the back of a spoon (see page 12). Season with salt and pepper.

5. Meanwhile, bring a large pot of salted water to boil. Add 12 tortelloni; remove when they float to the top.

6. Toss pasta in sauce and sprinkle with Parmesan cheese.

CLOSER LOOK *To make fresh tortelloni dough, like Chef Jason does at Ottimo Café, begin with any basic pasta dough (there's one on page 185). Roll out the dough on #2 setting, or until nearly paper-thin. Use a 3-inch round ring cutter to cut as many circles as you can out of the dough. Discard scraps. Place a damp cloth over circles until ready to use.*

TIDBIT *Chef Jason cooked at owner Akiva Reiner's home for one week before taking the helm at Ottimo.*

"A great chef keeps dishes simple yet exciting, and maintains the original qualities of the ingredients."

– CHEF JASON CAPPETTA, OTTIMO CAFÉ

CANNELLONI

MAXIM

OWNER/CHEF
Owner Moshe Nahari

LOCATION
The Golders Green area of London, England

Maxim, in the northwest section of London, is a private and cozy spot, complete with modern and comfy purple couches. Maxim, with a large following, is a neighborhood mainstay with both a "milky" (as the British would say) menu — including fish, quiches, pizzas — and Thai-inspired selections.

Our London friends love the Mushroom Risotto, which includes mushrooms and asparagus with risotto rice in a creamy wine sauce, the Stuffed Portobello Mushrooms, and the Salmon Stir-Fry.

The restaurant is also family-friendly. Order pizza to go, and you'll get another pie for free. Or, reserve the party room in the back to celebrate your occasion. There seem to be lots of reasons to keep coming back, including this flavorful Cannelloni, which is true comfort food. -L.

CANNELLONI

YIELD *8 servings*

CATEGORY *dairy*

DESCRIPTION
Pasta layers rolled with basil, cheese, and asparagus, topped with tomato sauce and melted cheese

To serve pretty individual portions of this dish, bake three cannelloni together in each small crock, as shown in the photo.

INGREDIENTS

1 *(1-LB)*	box lasagna sheets
3 CUPS	ricotta cheese
2 TBSP	fresh minced basil
2	garlic cloves, *crushed*
1½ TSP	kosher salt
20	asparagus spears, *trimmed*
4 CUPS	marinara sauce
8 OZ	shredded cheese

INSTRUCTIONS

1 Preheat oven to 390°F.

2 Prepare pasta according to package instructions. After lasagna is cooked, spread pasta on a greased baking sheet to prevent strands from sticking together.

3 In a medium bowl, combine ricotta cheese, basil, garlic, and salt. Place a heaping teaspoon of the ricotta mixture and 1 asparagus spear at the end of each lasagna sheet. Roll up (you may trim spears or leave them sticking out at the sides). Place lasagna roll-ups into a baking dish.

4 Top lasagna roll-ups with sauce and sprinkle with cheese. Bake, uncovered, for 20 minutes.

CLOSER LOOK *Out of ricotta? Make your own. Bring 1 gallon whole milk barely to a simmer. Stir in ⅔ cup vinegar. Let sit for a few minutes as the curds separate. Line a colander with paper towels. Transfer cheese curds to the colander and let drain until the ricotta cheese firms up, about 30 minutes.*

TIDBIT *While on an official visit to the Jewish community in Golders Green, London, then-British Prime Minister Margaret Thatcher stopped for coffee at this restaurant.*

RIGATONI MELANZANA

my most favorite food™

MY MOST FAVORITE FOOD

OWNER/CHEF
Owner Doris Schechter

NEW YORK CITY

LOCATION
The Upper West Side neighborhood of Manhattan, New York

Doris Schechter was just a baby when her family fled from Vienna after the Nazis came into power during World War II. Her family lived in Italy until they were among the 982 refugees chosen to board the *U.S.S. Henry Gibbons* and brought to Oswego, New York's Fort Ontario (the only refugees allowed into the United States during the war). Though she was still only six years old when the family moved to the Bronx, Doris grew up with the culinary legacy of her Viennese grandmother, who joined the family in New York. (Doris pays homage to her grandmother's delicacies in her book, *Oma's Table*.)

In 1982, Doris tapped that legacy and shared passion into a bakery called My Most Favorite Dessert Company, first based in Great Neck, New York, then in Manhattan, where Doris expanded her line of baked goods to include a café and a dinner menu. Now run by Doris's daughter Dena and her husband, Scott Magram, the bakery and café on the Upper West Side is still a spot to pick up desserts, such as peanut butter mousse cake, sour cream coffee cake, lemon pound cake, or the popular muffins (like the apple nut raisin). Order them to go or to savor in the restaurant along with a cappuccino … or enjoy lunch in the glass atrium garden room. The restaurant is even kashered completely before Passover, and offers a full line of kosher-for-Passover dishes (when you'll enjoy spaghetti squash with pesto). During the year, start your meal with the tomato soup and fresh café entrées like this Rigatoni Melanzana ("eggplant" in Italian). - V.

RIGATONI MELANZANA

YIELD *2 servings*

CATEGORY *dairy*

DESCRIPTION

Rigatoni pasta tossed with a creamy house tomato sauce, roasted eggplant, fresh basil, and fresh mozzarella cubes

You'll need to double the other ingredients if you're preparing a 1-pound box of rigatoni.

INGREDIENTS

¼ CUP	olive oil
1 CUP	*(1-inch dice)* eggplant
2	garlic cloves, *sliced*
½ TSP	kosher salt, *plus more to taste*
•	pinch coarse black pepper, *plus more to taste*
•	pinch dried oregano
1 CUP	uncooked rigatoni pasta
1½ CUPS	tomato sauce
2 TBSP	heavy cream *(optional)*
5	leaves fresh basil, *half chopped, half torn by hand*
1 TBSP	grated Parmesan cheese
¼ CUP	cubes fresh Mozzarella

INSTRUCTIONS

1 Heat olive oil in a frying pan over medium heat. Add eggplant, garlic, salt, pepper, and oregano. Sauté until eggplant is soft, 6-8 minutes. Alternatively, you can roast the eggplant: Toss eggplant with oil and seasonings on a baking sheet; bake at 350°F for 10-12 minutes.

2 Prepare pasta according to package instructions.

3 In a sauté pan over medium-high heat, combine eggplant, tomato sauce, and heavy cream. Bring to a simmer; cook for 4 minutes. Stir in rigatoni and chopped basil. Taste and add salt and pepper as necessary.

4 Add Parmesan and mozzarella cheese. Serve immediately, topped with torn basil leaves.

Rigatoni is tube-style pasta, larger than penne or ziti. It is most often ridged, which helps hold the sauce. The edges are square-cut, rather than angled like penne. We used rigatoni ziti, which is a little longer and narrower. Any tube-style pasta, preferably ridged, will work in this recipe.

"Since my formative years were spent living in a small city in Italy, with a father who was Orthodox and never compromised his dietary laws, I was inspired to open a kosher restaurant. Cooking means recapturing that taste of my early childhood."

- DORIS SCHECHTER, MY MOST FAVORITE RESTAURANT

ROSÉ PASTA

YIELD 4-6 servings

CATEGORY dairy

DESCRIPTION

Pasta, tossed in a light pink sauce made from fresh tomatoes, topped with basil and pine nuts

Pasta with a tomato-and-cream- based sauce is still perhaps the most popular pasta dish ordered in dairy restaurants. We loved the fresh version served at London's **SOYO**, *first featured on page 106.* **SOYO** *is known for making dishes healthier. This dish features a rich and flavorful sauce, without canned tomatoes and half the amount of cream usually found in pink sauces. Sun-dried tomato paste is a great secret ingredient.*

Don't skip the step of peeling the tomatoes. There are two methods: You can cut an "X" incision into the base of the tomato. Drop tomato into boiling water until "X" begins to split open, 20-30 seconds. Remove immediately and place into ice water. Beginning from the "X," pull skin gently away, Or, simply use a peeler to peel a firm tomato.

INGREDIENTS

¼ CUP	olive oil
6	garlic cloves, *chopped*
2 LB	fresh plum tomatoes, *peeled and cubed*
2 TBSP	sun-dried tomato paste
½	cup heavy cream
•	kosher salt, *to taste*
•	freshly ground black pepper, *to taste*
1 LB	penne or gemelli pasta
•	fresh basil leaves
•	roasted pine nuts
•	Parmesan shavings

INSTRUCTIONS

1 Heat olive oil in a saute pan over low heat. Add garlic and cook, 1-2 minutes. Add tomatoes and sun-dried tomato paste. Continue to cook for 45 minutes over low heat.

2 Transfer to a blender; blend until smooth. Return to pot; stir in cream. Season with salt and pepper to taste.

3 Meanwhile, prepare pasta al dente according to package instructions.

4 After draining pasta, stir into sauce. Mix well. Add fresh basil leaves. Plate and garnish with roasted pine nuts and Parmesan shavings.

FETTUCCINE TRI FUNGHI

CINE CITTA

CINE CITTA

OWNER/CHEF
Owners Dan Mamou & Frank Taieb / Chef Romulo De Melo

LOCATION
Surfside, Florida

FLORIDA

Cine Citta is synonymous with good times in Miami. Walk by and you'll always see happy diners in sunglasses sitting at the outdoor tables, sipping white wine while enjoying a wood-oven pizza Margarita or a Citta salad. It's just as much fun to be inside the sleek interior, as you lounge on the white leather bench seats.

Vacation. Sunny weather. Family and friends. Comforting, dairy gourmet Italian food. In a hip and modern atmosphere that's upscale without being stuffy.

The whole feel of Cine Citta is very European, and though the owners are from Paris, the restaurant is very serious about its Italian food. The pasta is all freshly made and the menu is in Italian (the food descriptions are in English).

Start with some antipasto (the traditional first course of an Italian meal), such as the crispy and creamy Mozzarella Fritta (fried rounds of fresh mozzarella cheese over fresh tomato sauce) or the Portobelli Ripieni (stuffed with ricotta, spinach, and artichoke over a red pepper coulis … yum).

There is a serious selection of fish entrées, creamy risottos, great brick-oven pizza, and homemade desserts. Those who want the authentic Italian experience, though, go for the pasta. And this Fettuccine Tri Funghi, a more gourmet version of its sister dish, Fettuccine Alfredo, is the most popular. - V.

FETTUCCINE TRI FUNGHI

YIELD *1 large serving*

CATEGORY *dairy*

DESCRIPTION

Fettuccine served with porcini, Portobello, and button mushrooms in cream sauce

It's recommended to first soak dried porcini mushrooms in hot water for 15 minutes and drain before adding to a dish. That flavorful soaking liquid is great to use in sauces or soups in place of water or stock. For more on dried porcini mushrooms, see page 15.

CLOSER LOOK *Whenever wine, or any alcohol, is added to a sauce, let it reduce for a little bit before adding the other liquids. This technique will help preserve the flavor and aroma the wine adds, while helping to eliminate the alcohol taste.*

INGREDIENTS

6 OZ	fettuccine
1 TBSP	butter
1	Portobello mushroom, *sliced, gills removed*
4	button mushrooms, *sliced*
1 SMALL	shallot, *chopped*
1 OZ	dried porcini mushrooms
¼ CUP	white wine
2½ CUPS	heavy cream
•	kosher salt, *to taste*
•	coarse black pepper, *to taste*
2 TBSP	grated Parmesan cheese

INSTRUCTIONS

1. Prepare pasta according to package instructions.

2. Melt butter in a sauté pan over low heat. Add Portobello mushroom, button mushrooms, and shallot; cook until tender, about 7-10 minutes. Add porcini mushrooms and white wine; cook additional 2 minutes. Add cream and cook until sauce thickens, 2-3 minutes. Season with salt and pepper.

3. Toss the pasta in the sauce; sprinkle with Parmesan cheese.

PIZZA DE NONNA

Everyone loves pizza, so why not make pizza better? That's what the three Sarway brothers thought when they set out to make a gourmet version of America's favorite place to eat: the neighborhood pizza shop.

Posh Tomato is the spot to satisfy even the most spoiled pizza lover's taste buds. The signature crust is the thinnest and crispiest anywhere, and the variations lure regulars back into one of Posh's hip locations to try each one.

Options begin with Italian-inspired pies, like this popular De Nonna or the Mushroom Truffle pizza with fresh mozzarella, goat cheese, Portobello mushrooms, fresh basil, and a drizzle of white truffle oil. Globally inspired pies include the Mediterranean, topped with za'atar, kalamata olives, plum tomatoes, a blend of cheeses, and a dollop of labne cheese.

The part of the menu that gets us the most excited, though, is dessert: Sweet pizzas include options like Chocolate S'mores, Cheesecake (with chocolate chips, cinnamon dust, and dulce de leche), or Banana Butter (flambéed with rum and Chantilly whipped cream) … it's all perfect on top of that thin, crispy crust. - V.

POSH *Tomato*

POSH TOMATO

OWNER/CHEF
The Sarway Brothers

LOCATION
2 locations in the Flatbush neighborhood of Brooklyn, NY

NEW YORK CITY

PIZZA DE NONNA

YIELD
4 personal pizzas

CATEGORY dairy

DESCRIPTION
Thin-crust pizza with a cheese blend, house sauce, house pesto sauce, and a dash of Parmesan cheese. Pizza de Nonna means "Grandmother's Pizza."

You'll notice that 90 grams is a very small amount. For a Posh-like pizza, make sure to weigh your dough and roll it really thin.
If you buy pizza dough from your local shop, it should make about 8 personal pizzas. One pound of frozen dough will make about 5.

Why does the sauce go on after the cheese? See Techniques on page 11.

Make it "Posh" — garnish with a sprinkle of oregano and a dash of garlic oil.

INGREDIENTS

10-12	spinach leaves
2 BUNCHES	fresh basil, *leaves only*
4-5	walnuts
2	garlic cloves
1 TSP	kosher salt
⅛ TSP	black pepper
1-2 TBSP	extra virgin olive oil
3 TBSP	canola oil
4	*(90 gram)* balls pizza dough
•	semolina flour, *for dusting*
8 OZ	shredded pizza cheese
4 TBSP	Parmesan cheese
1 CUP	pizza sauce

INSTRUCTIONS

1. Preheat oven to 500°F or 550°F.

2. Prepare the pesto: In a food processor, blend spinach, basil, walnuts, garlic, salt, and pepper; drizzle in oils, with motor running, until combine.

3. Prepare pizzas: Let dough balls rest for at least 10 minutes. On parchment paper dusted with semolina flour, roll each ball to a 9-inch circle.

4. Sprinkle with pizza cheese; dot with pizza sauce and pesto. Transfer parchment paper with pizza to a pizza stone or heavy baking sheet. Bake until golden and cheese is melted, 5-7 minutes. Sprinkle with Parmesan cheese and serve.

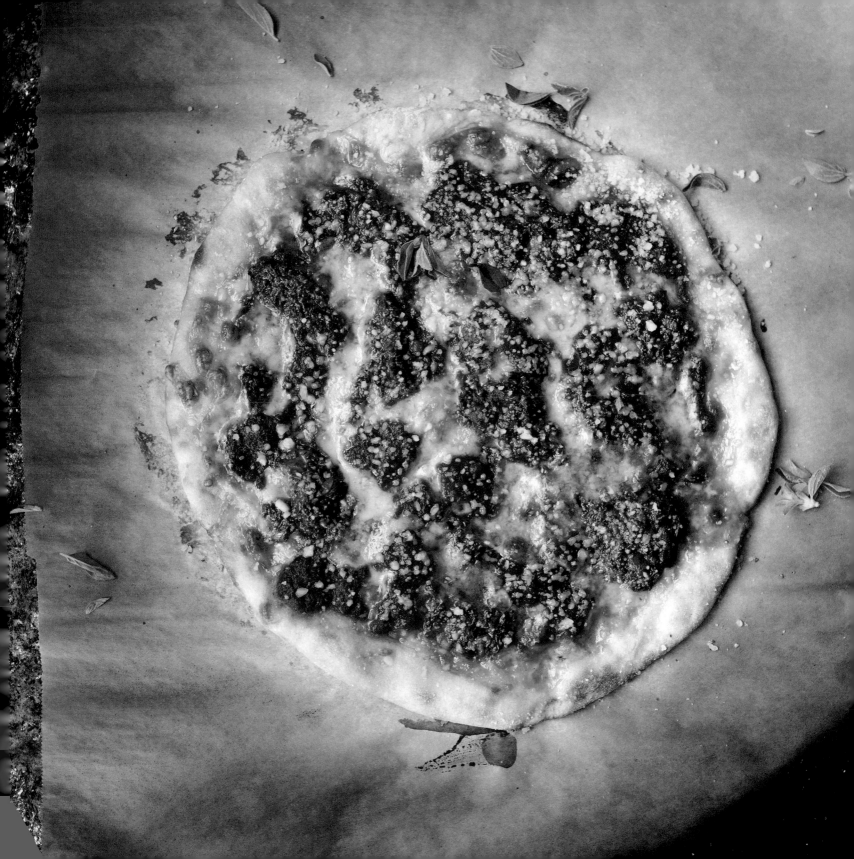

VEGETABLE & FETA CHEESE FOCACCIA

RICOTTA

LOCATION
Jerusalem, Israel

Situated away from the tourist areas in Jerusalem's high-tech district at the entrance to Har Hotzvim, Ricotta is where Jerusalem residents can escape to enjoy a quiet evening, enjoying Italian-style dishes, such as freshly baked pizzas and focaccia, pasta and gnocchi, fish, and salads … along with a panoramic view of the city.

The restaurant is busy, though, way before you arrive for dinner. It's open from 8 a.m. to accommodate the working people in the area, and is the go-to spot to treat your clients for breakfast or to have a business meeting over lunch. There's a spacious outdoor patio where you can enjoy drinks — or sip your morning latte.

Special dishes include hot salads, like the Toscana (which includes zucchini and mushrooms cooked in butter, garlic, and white wine, served with mixed greens and Parmesan cheese) or the Sweet Potato & Haloumi Salad (the potatoes and cheese are fried, glazed in date honey, and tossed with mixed greens, julienned apple, sesame seeds, and walnuts).

Other favorites include the fried Haloumi Cheese Sticks, the Bruschetta (served with a trio of different toppings including smoked salmon, aioli, and capers; tomato and basil; and ricotta with grilled eggplant), and the Panna Cotta or Belgian waffles for dessert.

To start the meal, though, most tables enjoy the Focaccia, which is served hot and crisp, topped with the season's best and freshest produce. - **L**.

VEGETABLE & FETA CHEESE FOCACCIA

YIELD *6 focaccias*

CATEGORY *dairy*

DESCRIPTION

Seasoned focaccia bread with sautéed vegetables and feta

At Ricotta, the vegetables served on top of the focaccia are adjusted according to what's in season. The chef also recommends adding black or green olives.

INGREDIENTS

FOCACCIA DOUGH:

2 CUPS	lukewarm water
2 TBSP	instant yeast
¼ CUP	sugar
6-7 CUPS	flour
¼ CUP	olive oil
1 TBSP	kosher salt

TOPPING:

2 TBSP	oil
1	onion, *cut into wedges*
1	red bell pepper, *thinly sliced*
1 PINT	cherry tomatoes
½ TSP	kosher salt
•	olive oil, *for drizzling*
•	coarse salt, *for sprinkling*
•	pinch coarse black pepper
•	fresh or dried rosemary, *for sprinkling*
4 OZ	Bulgarian or feta cheese, *coarsely crumbled*

INSTRUCTIONS

1 In the bowl of an electric mixer fitted with a dough hook, combine water, yeast, sugar, and a pinch of flour. Add in oil, remaining flour (begin with 6 cups total; add up to 7 if necessary), and salt; knead until smooth. Cover with a towel and let rise 1½ hours.

2 Flour a surface to roll out the dough (it will be sticky). Divide dough into 6 pieces and roll into circles or ovals. Place on parchment paper. Cover and let rise an additional 30 minutes.

3 Preheat oven to 475°F.

4 Meanwhile, prepare the topping: Heat oil in a sauté pan over medium heat. Add onion, bell pepper, tomatoes, salt, and pepper; cook for 3-4 minutes.

5 Drizzle rolled-out dough with olive oil, coarse salt, pepper, and rosemary. Prick with a fork. Top with sautéed vegetables and feta cheese. Bake for 12 minutes.

Bulgarian cheese, commonly found in Israel, is a type of feta cheese. Feta cheese commonly found in the U.S. is usually the Greek variety. Although Bulgarian cheese is firmer and creamier (Greek feta is easier to crumble), use them interchangeably.

Another fun way to serve this is to bake the focaccia with olive oil, salt, pepper, and rosemary for 9-11 minutes. Serve freshly grilled vegetables or salad on top.

SPINACH QUICHE

Haroa BaCafe
Coffee Restaurant

HAROA BACAFÉ

OWNER/CHEF
Owned by The Shikler Family / Chef Harel Sulam

LOCATION
Kfar Haro'eh, a moshav in Israel

Haroa BaCafé was my husband's grandmother's pick when we asked her about her favorite Israeli restaurant to visit. For generations, the site of Haroa BaCafé was the Shikler family's farm, which included an orange grove, a chicken coop, and cows at pasture. The farm was built by the family patriarch to be a source of income for the family, back in the days when the town of Kfar Haro'eh (a *moshav* near the coast, north of Netanya) was established.

Today, the café sits in the midst of the orange grove (sit outdoors, under the fruit-filled branches). You'll agree that the Haroa BaCafé experience is completely different from a meal at any city café. Does food taste better when you're breathing in pure air and listening to birds sing? Or could it simply be the freshness of the straight-from-the-farm ingredients? (Even the cheese is made in the *moshav!*) Yes and yes.

Haroa BaCafé is a family business, managed by the Shikler family. The service is personal and attentive; the atmosphere is the epitome of calm. Before you order, make sure to save room for desserts (or take one home; there's also a bakery). Begin the meal with fresh, warm bread spread with garlic butter, sip a latte or "café hafoch," and enjoy a salad, pasta, soup, or one of the popular freshly prepared quiches (new varieties are made daily), such as this one. -**L.**

SPINACH QUICHE

YIELD *1 quiche*

CATEGORY *dairy*

DESCRIPTION

Fresh spinach and cheese baked in a flaky, buttery crust

After 15 years in business, Haroa BaCafé underwent renovation while preserving all of its charm. Along with the renovation came a brand-new menu

INGREDIENTS

QUICHE CRUST:

2¾ CUPS	*(350 grams)* flour
14 TBSP	*(200 grams or 1¾ cups)* cold butter, *diced*
½ CUP	*(100 grams)* sour cream
¼ TSP	kosher salt
1 TSP	baking powder

FILLING:

3 TBSP	oil, *for sautéing*
1	onion, *diced*
1	leek, *white and light green parts, diced*
•	pinch salt
18 OZ	*(500 grams)* fresh spinach
3	eggs
7 OZ	*(200 grams)* shredded Mozzarella cheese
3½ OZ	*(100 grams)* feta cheese
1 TBSP	flour
•	pinch coarse black pepper
•	pinch nutmeg

INSTRUCTIONS

1 Prepare the crust: In the bowl of an electric mixer, combine flour, butter, sour cream, salt, and baking powder. Let rest for 30 minutes at room temperature. Divide dough into two uneven pieces (one ¾ and one ¼ of the dough). Press the larger piece of dough into bottom and up the sides of a pie dish; prick with a fork. Place remaining dough in the refrigerator until ready to use.

2 Preheat oven to 350°F.

3 Prepare the filling: Heat oil in a sauté pan over medium heat. Add onion, leek, and salt; sauté for 5-7 minutes. Add spinach and continue to cook for 5 minutes. Transfer contents to a strainer to drain excess liquid.

4 In a large bowl, combine drained spinach mixture, eggs, Mozzarella cheese, feta cheese, flour, salt, pepper, and nutmeg. Grate remaining ¼ piece of dough over the top, like a crumble. Bake for 45 minutes.

TIDBIT *When it became difficult to rely on agricultural income, Shoshanna Shikler, the mother of the four Shikler brothers, began baking and selling cakes. Her bakery, the first non-agricultural business in the moshav, became very popular. All the freshly made desserts at Haroa BaCafé are prepared by Shoshanna.*

A tart or pie pan with a removable bottom is the best choice to use with this recipe. While the café makes round quiches, we used a 9-inch square tart pan for an updated look.

PIZAZA MILKSHAKES

PIZAZA

PIZAZA

OWNER/CHEF

Owner Lee Landau / Chef Elad Asnafi

LOCATION

Hendon and Golders Green, London, England

PIZAZA is London's favorite spot to enjoy pizza, milkshakes, and their famous chili fries. The atmosphere is bright, the service is quick and friendly, and decor is hip — and the food is much more interesting than in your traditional pizza shop.

PIZAZA understands that pizza is a very personal thing and lets you customize your pie. Choose your crust style. (Do you like it thin and crispy, Italian-style? Deep-dish? Stuffed crust? Or thin and whole wheat?) Choose from 15 topping combinations and the perfect amount of cheese and spice. (You can also choose a dip for extra fun and no extra charge.)

The Golders Green location is also a great place for a family outing. (The PIZAZA in Hendon is quieter and more appropriate for your business lunch meeting.) There are wall-mounted computers at the tables, where you can order from a digital menu (or choose to have waiter service instead), play games, chat to other tables, draw digital images, or take photos of all the people at your table to email to yourself or others. When the kids are entertained, the whole meal becomes a very enjoyable experience.

All this fun and we didn't even get to the milkshake menu yet, which is extensive, with a shake to match every type of candy bar (almost as fun to read as it is to drink one). Here are two of the most popular. -**L**.

PIZAZA MILKSHAKES

YIELD *1 large serving*

CATEGORY *dairy*

DESCRIPTION

A refreshing and simple blend of strawberries and ice cream; PIZAZA's signature chocolate cookie shake with caramelized pecans

Like your milkshakes extra chilled and wonderfully creamy for longer? Place your glasses in the fridge for at least 60 minutes before serving.

STRAWBERRIES AND CREAM MILKSHAKE

INGREDIENTS

⅔ CUP	milk *(whole or lowfat)*
1¼ CUPS	soft vanilla ice cream
4-6	strawberries
¾ OZ	*(4 squares)* white chocolate

TOPPINGS:

- whipped cream
- 1 strawberry, *sliced*

INSTRUCTIONS

1 In the jar of a blender, combine milk, ice cream, strawberries, and white chocolate. Blend until smooth.

2 Pour into a milkshake glass. Top with whipped cream and strawberry slices, optional.

THE PIZAZA SHAKE

INGREDIENTS

⅔ CUP	milk *(whole or lowfat)*
1¼ CUP	soft vanilla ice cream
¾ OZ	*(4 squares)* white chocolate
2	chocolate sandwich cookies
4-6	caramelized pecans
1	squeeze vanilla or French vanilla syrup

INSTRUCTIONS

1 In the jar of a blender, combine milk, ice cream, white chocolate, cookies, pecans, and syrup. Blend until smooth.

2 Pour into a milkshake glass and serve.

CARAMELIZED PECANS

Caramelized pecans are readily available on grocery store shelves, but PIZAZA caramelizes its own. Here's how it's done:

1 Add 2½ cups pecans to a saucepan. Cover with boiling water, 2 heaping tablespoons sugar, and 1½ tablespoons honey. Let simmer for 20 minutes, stirring occasionally to prevent the sugar from sticking to the bottom of the pot.

2 Strain to remove excess liquid. Spread pecans on a tray to dry completely.

3 In a small saucepan, heat oil to 350°F. Using a straining spoon, carefully lower the pecans into the hot oil for 30 seconds. Remove to a paper towel-lined bowl and let cool.

CLOSER LOOK

To get that authentic milkshake flavor at home, we used vanilla syrup, similar to what you'd use to flavor your latte (sold by brands such as Torani). Home cooks can use another trick to achieve that vanilla flavor: Use a spoonful of instant vanilla pudding powder.

Soft-serve ice cream is softer than regular ice cream because air is constantly being introduced as it freezes. Most commonly enjoyed at ice cream shops, it has recently become available in the freezer section of your grocery. If you can't find it, substitute hard vanilla ice cream.

CHINESE "TAKE-IN" NIGHT

MAIN

Mongolian Beef
(page 190)

OR

*Eggplant Chicken in
Garlic Sauce*
(page 124)

OR

Sesame Chicken
(page 148)

SIDE

Yakisoba Pan Noodles
(page 63)

HOLIDAY MEAL

STARTER

Eggplant Ghetto Style
(page 66)

OR

Cauliflower Bisque
(page 80)

MAIN

Bourbon BBQ Ribs
(page 172)

OR

*Chinese-Style Glazed
Corned Beef (page 176)*

OR

Slow-Cooked Okinawa Ribs
(page 180)

OR

Osso Buco
(page 186)

DESSERT

Chocolate Babka Bread Pudding
(page 262)

DESSERTS

"THERE'S ALWAYS ROOM FOR SOMETHING SWEET."
~Talmud, Eruvin 82b

FINANCIERS

PARDES

OWNER/CHEF
Owner/Chef Moshe Wendel

LOCATION
Downtown Brooklyn, New York

Chef Wendel deserves the distinction of the number-one out-of-the-box thinker in kosher. Pardes is your destination when you want to taste something exciting. I never really understood when people used the term "mind-blowing" to describe food until I ate there. Each plate is a work of art, and the flavors defy convention, but work so magnificently well together. If you look around the restaurant, you'll see people really, really enjoying themselves.

More of our foodie friends describe the experience very well.

Shoshy: "Love it! The menu is always changing and the food is always beautiful and exciting. I can always look forward to favorites there or finding something new to try. It's where I overcame my fear of trying something new. Eating at Pardes also teaches me about food pairings, and what would work well together that I might never have thought of. And contrary to what people think, it's not so expensive."

Melinda: "He pairs foods together that you would have never thought would match — but they do, incredibly. Make sure to finish everything on your plate, because there's a reason for every component."

When ordering, think of items on the menu as snacks. Order many items to share so you can experience a variety. And the food doesn't come out in a specific order. Be aware to let go of conventional expectations when you eat at Pardes.

Dessert is out-of-control tasty. Here's a taste of one of them. Chef Wendel tells us, "This is a simple cake that's used as a base for more complex desserts." He also recommends enjoying it simply with berries and whipped cream. Or try the dairy version: "Substitute oil with melted butter or better yet … brown butter." - V.

FINANCIERS

YIELD *12 mini cakes*

CATEGORY *pareve*

DESCRIPTION

A light and moist French cake

You'll have perfect results every time when you measure your ingredients by weight instead of volume, so if you own a digital scale, use it! If you don't own one, here are some approximate measurements: 100 grams flour is ⅘-cup; 100 grams ground almonds is 1 cup; 300 grams sugar is 1½ cups plus 1 tablespoon; 150 grams oil is ⅔-cup.

INGREDIENTS

8	egg whites
300 GRAMS	sugar
100 GRAMS	flour
100 GRAMS	almond flour OR ground almonds
•	pinch kosher salt
150 GRAMS	canola oil

INSTRUCTIONS

1 Preheat oven to 350°F. Grease 12 (4-ounce) ramekins with nonstick baking spray.

2 In the bowl of an electric mixer, beat egg whites until foamy. Slowly add sugar and beat until stiff peaks form.

3 Fold in flour, almond flour, and salt. Then fold in oil.

4 Portion batter into prepared ramekins. Bake for 18 minutes.

5 Let cool. Flip cakes onto serving plate and sprinkle with confectioners' sugar.

TIDBIT *Pardes was originally supposed to be called "Lavender." They went from one plant to many by using the name "Pardes," which means "Orchard" in Hebrew.*

Chef Wendel uses Heckers All-Purpose Flour.

"Taste before you serve; you're almost never using enough salt. Cook what's in season and buy from local farmers. Buy one good knife, preferably Japanese, and keep it sharp."

- CHEF MOSHE WENDEL, PARDES.

NAPOLEON

THE LOFT STEAKHOUSE

OWNER/CHEF
Executive Chef Boris Poleschuk

LOCATION
The Borough Park neighborhood of Brooklyn, New York

I was invited to come and enjoy The Loft experience soon after it opened. First, let's talk about the atmosphere, because that's a "whoa," especially when you're stepping off the streets of Borough Park. The restaurant, with exposed brick walls and glass water fountain in the back, feels like a slice of Soho. It's the perfect place to feel like you're getting away when you don't have time to go far.

Those at our table got to taste the range of The Loft's appetizers and entrees … Chicken Lollipops to Sweetbreads and Grilled Steak Salad, then Pan-Roasted Loft Chicken, a side of creamy parsnip mash, and the Signature Cut steak with a bourbon glaze. Eating was fun, but I really wanted to go back and watch Executive Chef Boris Poleschuk in action (what's a good meal without a learning a new cooking tip?) … and I did.

The cherry, though, really came with dessert. I expect dairy desserts to be awesome. That's not a feat. But I didn't expect this pareve Napoleon to be awesome. I could have eaten this cream endlessly. I needed to know how they make it. And now I do. -**V.**

NAPOLEON

YIELD *12 napoleons*

CATEGORY *pareve*

DESCRIPTION

Layers of crisp pastry and custard

During the photo shoot, our friend, pastry chef Margie Schreck, popped in and gave us a tip for getting the pastry dough thin and crisp in a home oven. After rolling, place the pastry dough between two heavy sheet pans to bake (with parchment paper over and under the dough).

INGREDIENTS

CUSTARD:

5	egg yolks
6 TBSP	sugar
1 TBSP	cornstarch
2 CUPS	coconut milk
1 TSP	vanilla extract
¼ TSP	orange extract
•	pinch cayenne pepper
•	pinch kosher salt
1 TSP	lemon zest
1½ CUPS	nondairy whipped topping

PASTRY LEAVES:

36	*(3-inch)* puff pastry squares
2	egg whites
1 CUP	sanding sugar

INSTRUCTIONS

1. Prepare the custard: In the bowl of an electric mixer, beat yolks with sugar and cornstarch until fluffy.

2. In a saucepan over medium-high heat, combine coconut milk, vanilla extract, orange extract, cayenne pepper, salt, and lemon zest. Bring to a boil. Strain mixture through a sieve. Slowly pour coconut milk into yolks. (See Techniques, page 10.)

3. Whip nondairy whipped topping until stiff. Fold into yolk/coconut milk mixture. Let settle and chill for 6 hours or overnight. Cream will last for up to a week, refrigerated.

4. Prepare the pastry leaves: Place squares on two parchment-lined baking sheets. (If using uncut pastry dough, roll out thinly on parchment paper and slice into 3-inch squares. Transfer parchment and squares to baking sheet). Brush with egg whites and cover generously with sanding sugar. Top each baking sheet with a piece of parchment paper and an additional baking sheet. Bake for 25 minutes.

5. To serve, add some of the custard filling into a pastry bag fitted with a star tip. Pipe a small amount of custard onto a plate to secure the first pastry leaf. Pipe a layer of cream on top, and continue to layer pastry leaves and custard.

TIDBIT *At the Loft, Napoleons are assembled just before serving. Home cooks who like to prepare ahead, though, can assemble the Napoleons and keep them frozen until ready to serve.*

At The Loft, the Napoleons usually have three layers, and are piped using a jumbo star tip. We gave you a few extra layers.

"There are some things that are a match made in heaven. Salty and sweet is one of them. If your dessert or pastry doesn't call for salt, be brave enough to add a pinch. Salt enhances every flavor, and it'll give your desserts a whole new dimension."

– SOUS-CHEF AVIVA EMANUEL, THE LOFT STEAKHOUSE

CRÈME BRÛLÉE

Delicatessen

WOLF & LAMB

Steakhouse

WOLF AND LAMB

OWNER/CHEF
Owner Zalman Wuensch

LOCATION
The Midwood neighborhood of Brooklyn; Midtown Manhattan, New York

NEW YORK CITY

Since Wolf & Lamb has locations in both the heart of Midwood and Midtown Manhattan, making it very accessible to lots of family and friends, we had to consider so many opinions when it came to deciding which of the restaurant's elevated and special dishes to feature.

"The Lamb Sliders are scrumptious." (Everyone talks about these sliders … everyone.)

"I had the Grilled Hangar Steak Tacos for an appetizer … with shredded beef, red onion, avocado, jalapeño, and cilantro …."

"The Bourbon Pecan Bread Pudding! I want to make it for Friday night … or the S'Mores."

"The Natural Roasted Chicken … the first one on the menu, the one that comes with fingerling potatoes … it's so unbelievably good, it's scary."

Our friend Marnie Levy, though, didn't let me choose from all these suggestions. She said we must feature the pareve crème brûlée. Why? Because she never tasted a good pareve crème brûlée until she had it at Wolf & Lamb. "They also make a maple syrup version which is so aromatic."

I agreed. And because I, too, was on a search for fabulous parve crème brûlée, Marnie then went to visit the chef at the Midwood location to learn the secrets. I no longer need to wait 'til I'm serving a dairy meal to enjoy my favorite dessert. - **V**.

CRÈME BRÛLÉE

YIELD *12 servings*

CATEGORY *pareve*

DESCRIPTION

Baked custard topped with caramelized sugar

You can also make crème brûlée in a silicone mold for a different type of presentation. Unmold before torching.

INGREDIENTS

2 CUPS	nondairy creamer
1	vanilla bean, *scraped*
½ CUP	sugar
•	zest of 1 citrus fruit *(orange, blood orange, lemon, or Meyer lemon)*
9	egg yolks
•	granulated sugar, *for sprinkling*

INSTRUCTIONS

1 Preheat oven to 325°F.

2 Add creamer to a medium saucepan over medium heat. Add vanilla bean, sugar, and zest; heat to 170°F.

3 In a large bowl, whisk egg yolks. Then, whisking rapidly, slowly add in the hot liquid (see Techniques, page 10). Make sure not to scramble the eggs.

4 Prepare a water bath with ¼-inch hot water. Add ramekins to water bath and pour batter into each ramekin.

5 Bake for 25-30 minutes. (When you touch the middle and the batter doesn't cling to your finger, they're done. Deep ramekins will take longer to bake.) Chill overnight.

6 Sprinkle custard with granulated sugar. Torch until sugar is melted and golden.

CLOSER LOOK
For more on the process of tempering (slowly adding hot liquid to egg yolks), see Techniques on page 10.

To make the aromatic maple syrup variety, replace half the sugar with ¼ cup of pure maple syrup.

CHOCOLATE BABKA BREAD PUDDING

THE PRIME GRILL

OWNER/CHEF
Owner Joey Allaham/
Executive Chef David Kolotkin/
Pastry Chef Felencia Darius

LOCATION
Midtown
Manhattan,
New York

The Prime Grill, the original restaurant of the Prime Hospitality Group, is one restaurant that doesn't shy away from revealing its secrets.

Back in Syria, the Allaham family had been butchers for four generations. In 1993, when the family came to the United States and became familiar with the culture in Manhattan, Mr. Allaham had a vision: He would create an elegant atmosphere where businessmen and women — and all those who appreciate good food — could enjoy the high-quality meat he would offer.

That vision got across, because to me, The Prime Grill always meant "Tuesday night" and "Delmonico Steak." (Make sure to get there early.) The secret to that steak, though, was made public last year when *The Prime Grill Cookbook* was published, revealing the steak recipe and much more.

But restaurants evolve and add new dishes, and there are always new secrets for us to discover. And this one comes in the form of a really spectacular dessert. **- V.**

CHOCOLATE BABKA BREAD PUDDING

YIELD *14-16 ramekins*

CATEGORY *pareve*

DESCRIPTION

Slices of rich chocolate babka, baked in a vanilla custard and served warm with a scoop of ice cream

What kind of ice cream goes well over your bread pudding? Vanilla will always work, but The Prime Grill serves this next to a scoop of bourbon ice cream.

INGREDIENTS

½ CUP	nondairy creamer
¼ CUP	sugar, *divided*
2¼ TSP	*(1 packet)* active dry yeast
3 CUPS	all-purpose flour
•	pinch kosher salt
1 CUP	*(2 sticks)* cold margarine, *cut into pieces*
3	egg yolks

FILLING:

3	egg whites
½ CUP	sugar
1	*(12-oz)* can chocolate filling, *NOT frosting (see note)*

STREUSEL TOPPING:

3 TBSP	all-purpose flour
4 TBSP	sugar
2 TBSP	cold margarine, *cut into pieces*

CUSTARD:

3 CUPS	nondairy creamer
1 CUP	sugar, *divided*
½	vanilla bean *OR* 1 tsp. vanilla extract
3	egg yolks
2	eggs
•	pinch kosher salt

INSTRUCTIONS

1 In a medium saucepan, scald the creamer over low heat (small bubbles will form on the pan's sides). Let cool to 110°F. Stir in 1 tablespoon sugar and yeast. Let stand for 7 minutes, until bubbly.

2 Meanwhile, in the bowl of a food processor fitted with the metal blade (or by hand using a pastry blender), combine flour, salt, and remaining 3 tablespoons sugar, pulsing to blend. Pulse in the margarine as if for pie dough. Add egg yolks and yeast mixture; pulse until a ball of dough forms. Place into a clean bowl, cover with plastic wrap, and refrigerate several hours or overnight.

3 Place a rack in the center of the oven. Preheat oven to 350°F. Grease 2 (8½ x 4½-inch) loaf pans; set aside.

4 Prepare the filling: Beat egg whites until soft peaks form. Add sugar and whip until stiff peaks form. Reserve.

5 Prepare the streusel topping: Combine flour, sugar, and margarine until crumbs form.

6 Divide dough in half. (Keep one half refrigerated until ready to roll.) On a lightly floured surface or parchment paper, roll first half into a 12 x 18-inch rectangle. Spread dough with half the chocolate filling and then half

the whipped egg white mixture. Fold in the sides of dough and roll up as for a jellyroll. Fold in half, twist, and place in prepared pan. Sprinkle with half the streusel topping. Cover with greased plastic wrap and let rise until above the rim of the pan. Repeat with remaining dough.

7 Bake babka for about 40 minutes or until an instant-read thermometer registers 190°F. Let cool for 5 minutes in pan, then carefully turn out onto a rack to cool completely.

8 Prepare the custard: Heat creamer with ½ cup sugar in a medium saucepan over medium heat until scalded (you'll see small bubbles on the sides of the pan). Split the vanilla bean in half, if using, and scrape the seeds into the cream OR add the vanilla extract.

9 Meanwhile, in a medium bowl, combine egg yolks and eggs. Slowly whisk in remaining ½ cup sugar, then slowly whisk in hot cream. Strain the mixture through a fine sieve into a pitcher or measuring cup. Stir in the salt. Set aside.

10 Preheat oven to 300°F. Slice the babka. Fill individual ramekins with babka slices. Pour custard over babka. Bake for 15-20 minutes. Serve warm.

You'll find chocolate filling in the baking aisle. Unlike frosting, chocolate filling is meant to withstand high temperatures when baked, while frosting would run. The filling has a much thicker consistency than the frosting.

Do you have leftover babka? Make babka bread pudding by beginning with Step 8.

You can freeze the babka and custard. When ready to serve, defrost the custard, slice the babka, assemble, and bake fresh.

ZEPPOLI CINNAMON DOUGHNUTS

TIERRA SUR

OWNER/CHEF
Chef Gabriel Garcia

LOCATION
Herzog Winery, Oxnard, California

In the kosher restaurant world, we have our neighborhood favorites where we like to pick up something quickly. We have the places we'd go to when we want a nice night out, or want to celebrate a special occasion. But then there are the places that we dream about … and plan our vacations around.

Tierra Sur is off the beaten path, the middle of farm country at the Herzog Winery in Oxnard, California. It's about an hour from Los Angeles (without traffic), but its location says: This is worth the trip. Tierra Sur is considered one of the finest kosher restaurants in North America, possibly in the world.

Tierra Sur is a farm-to-table restaurant; it's small with an open kitchen, but very, very special. The menu changes with the seasons and the local crops. You can go for lunch and dinner on the same day and choose from an entirely different menu.

If you don't find one of your favorites on the main menu, like the Pulled BBQ Brisket Sliders with onion rings, look on the bar menu. Many of the dishes are inspired by the winery (the rib eye has an amazing grape reduction; the halibut has a red wine sabayon sauce). Other favorites include Green Bean Fries with a Smoky Tomato Sauce, Chorizo Lamb Sausages, and Fried Cornish Hens.

Oh, yes, when you eat at a winery, there's wine. When you order from the wine-tasting menu, your waiter will keep pouring and pouring. (Make sure you have someone to drive you home safely!)

And though you can't depend on ordering the same item you enjoyed last time, one thing you can depend on is dessert: these doughnuts are the Tierra Sur's signature sweet ending to a meal. Many people come just for these alone. - L.

ZEPPOLI CINNAMON DOUGHNUTS

YIELD *15 servings*

CATEGORY *pareve*

DESCRIPTION

Doughnut balls served with hot chocolate sauce

Sometimes Tierra Sur serves these churro-style, squeezing the dough through a piping bag directly into the hot oil.

INGREDIENTS

750 GRAMS	*(5½ cups)* flour
68 GRAMS	*(⅓ cup)* sugar
1 TSP	cinnamon
•	pinch kosher salt
2 CUPS	nondairy creamer
1 CUP	water
1½ TBSP	active dry yeast
2	eggs
1 TBSP	extra-virgin olive oil
•	oil, *for frying*

HOT CHOCOLATE SAUCE:

1 TBSP	cornstarch
•	cold water *(as needed)*
1 LB	chocolate, *chopped*
2 CUPS	sugar
½ CUP	brown sugar
2 CUPS	water
•	pinch cayenne pepper

CINNAMON-SUGAR MIXTURE:

•	cinnamon, *to taste*
2 CUPS	sugar

INSTRUCTIONS

1. In a large mixing bowl, sift together flour, sugar, cinnamon, and salt. Set aside.

2. In a small saucepan, combine nondairy creamer and water. Heat until warm (approximately 98°F). Remove from heat and whisk in yeast. Set aside to cool; mixture will foam.

3. In a small bowl, whisk together eggs and olive oil. Add to yeast mixture. Whisk the yeast mixture into dry ingredients until thoroughly combined. Allow dough to double in size, about 1-1 ½ hours.

4. Meanwhile, prepare the chocolate sauce: In a small bowl, combine cornstarch and enough cold water to form a smooth slurry. Set aside.

5. In a medium saucepan over medium heat, combine chocolate, sugar, brown sugar, and water. Whisk until mixture comes to a boil. Add cayenne pepper and cornstarch slurry to mixture; continuously whisk until sauce thickens slightly. Remove from heat and allow to cool.

6. Preheat fryer or a pot of oil to 350°F.

7. Meanwhile, prepare the cinnamon sugar mixture: Combine cinnamon and sugar in a shallow dish.

8. Working in batches, scoop out 1-tablespoon portions of dough and drop into hot oil. Cook until fritters are dark brown and a toothpick inserted in the middle comes out clean.

9. Transfer fritters to a paper towel or cooling rack to drain excess oil, about 1 minute. Toss fritters in cinnamon-sugar mixture. Serve with hot chocolate sauce.

For round doughnuts, we greased our hands so we could roll the dough into balls after scooping with a cookie scoop.

Even though we've given you the approximate cup equivalents, if you own a digital scale, measure your ingredients in grams for perfect zeppolis.

Before or after your meal at Tierra Sur, visit the winery's tasting room and take a tour of the Herzog's cellar, barrel room, and bottling line.

"The wise man learns from everyone. When it comes to food, everyone adds something to the pot, whether a chef or not."

– CHEF GABRIEL GARCIA, TIERRA SUR

CHOCOLATE SOUFFLÉ

CINE CITTA

It's hard to find a kosher restaurant that doesn't serve either a souffle or a molten cake for dessert. And though these hot chocolate indulgences topped with ice cream have long been popular, they're still the most frequently ordered desserts. This one comes from **CINE CITTA** *in Florida, the restaurant that brought us Fettuccine Tri Funghi on page 230.*

YIELD *2 servings*

CATEGORY *dairy*

DESCRIPTION

Light, springy chocolate souffle served with vanilla ice cream

INGREDIENTS

1 TBSP	unsalted butter, *plus more for coating ramekins*
2 TBSP	plus 2 tsp sugar, *plus more for coating ramekins, divided*
⅓ CUP	chopped semisweet chocolate
½ TSP	vanilla extract
•	pinch cinnamon
1 LARGE	egg yolk
1 TBSP	warm water
2 LARGE	egg whites, *at room temperature*
⅛ TSP	fresh lemon juice
•	pinch salt
•	confectioners' sugar
•	vanilla ice cream, *for serving*

INSTRUCTIONS

1 Grease 2 ramekins with softened butter; coat with sugar. Chill for at least 30 minutes in freezer.

2 With oven rack in lower third of the oven, preheat to 400°F.

3 In heatproof bowl set over a pan of simmering water, combine chocolate and 1 tablespoon butter. Stir occasionally, until melted and smooth. Remove from heat; stir in vanilla and cinnamon. Set aside.

4 Using an electric mixer, beat egg yolk and warm water until frothy. Slowly add 2 teaspoons sugar; beat for 5 minutes. Fold egg yolk into chocolate mixture.

5 Add egg whites to clean bowl of an electric mixer fitted with the whisk attachment. Add lemon juice and salt. Beat on medium speed until frothy, then gradually add 2 tablespoons sugar. Increase speed to high; beat until stiff peaks form.

6 Fold ⅓ egg white mixture into chocolate. Fold in remaining whites until just blended. Spoon into ramekins. Place ramekins on a baking sheet; bake until soufflé rises and when top springs back when touched with your finger, 15-20 minutes. Remove from oven; dust with confectioners' sugar. Serve immediately with ice cream.

PRALINE BROWNIES

www.bagelsngreens.com

BAGELS 'N GREENS

LOCATION

Three locations, including two in the Borough Park neighborhood and one in the Flatbush neighborhood of Brooklyn, New York.

NEW YORK CITY

Bagels 'n Greens is refreshing. Bright, green ... that's what I think of when I think about my BNG experiences. It's the ultimate café "take a break from the day" experience ... relaxing atmosphere (sit on the deck in the back of the original 18th Avenue location and you've left Brooklyn for a bit) ... the kind of fresh, natural food that you feel good about eating ... and lots of options to please the entire crew of friends, including those who want to stick to their diets and those who want to indulge.

The second aspect of the Bagels 'n Greens experience that I really enjoy is the ... pampering. The presentation of the food is very modern and a big part of the experience. The real pampering comes, though, when you receive a BNG gift basket. That's the ultra-cool gift you send when you want to make someone's day.

We've had requests to feature one of BNG's healthful recipes, like the low-cal zucchini soup, but this one aptly sums up that "pampering" aspect of the experience and BNG's sweets.

When Rebecca of BNG shared this recipe with us, she warned, "Wait until cool to cut (if you could wait ...). Don't forget to kiss your diet goodbye ...." - L.

PRALINE BROWNIES

DESCRIPTION

The richest, fudgiest brownies with bits of white chocolate and a praline glaze

After becoming the only kosher café using the Nespressio Aguila System, BNG served 35,000 cups of espresso over a nine-month period.

INGREDIENTS

8 oz	bittersweet chocolate
1 cup	*(2 sticks)* butter
4	eggs
1⅓ cups	*(11 oz)* sugar
1 cup	*(5 oz)* flour
½ cup	*(2 oz)* cocoa
½ tsp	kosher salt
1 tsp	nut extract *(optional)*
2 tsp	praline extract *(optional)*
7 oz	white chocolate, *coarsely chopped*

CHOCOLATE FROSTING:

10 oz	milk chocolate
4 Tbsp	praline paste

GARNISHES:

4 oz	mixed crunchy nuts

- chocolate and white chocolate curls

INSTRUCTIONS

1 Preheat oven to 350°F. Line a rimmed 9 x 13-inch baking sheet with parchment paper.

2 Melt chocolate with the butter.

3 In the bowl of an electric mixer, whip eggs and sugar at high speed for 5-6 minutes.

4 Carefully pour in melted chocolate mixture. Sift in flour, cocoa, and salt. Mix until mixture is smooth and shiny, about 4 minutes. Add in extracts, if using. Fold in white chocolate.

5 Pour batter into prepared baking sheet. Bake for 25 minutes (the edges should be hard, top cracked, and middle soft).

6 Prepare the frosting: Melt chocolate over a double boiler. Add praline paste and mix until combined. Gently pour over the top of the cake. Tilt the pan sideways until entire cake is fully covered. Sprinkle nuts or chocolate curls on top. Refrigerate for 15 minutes, until frosting is set. Let cool before slicing into bars.

TIDBIT *During the month of Chanukah, BNG sells over 55,000 donuts in 38 varieties.*

Praline paste is made from hazelnuts/ filberts and sugar, ground into a paste.

Bagels 'n Greens gets its produce fresh from the market every single morning. No tomato ever "slept" in the BNG kitchen overnight. Leftovers are donated to charity or needy families each day.

CEREAL MILK ICE CREAM

SERENDIPITY YOGURT CAFÉ

OWNER/CHEF
Owner Jessica Weiss

LOCATION
Surfside, Florida

Some people think that a great meal means a great steak. Others think that a great meal means awesome pizza or sushi. I think it's great ice cream.

When I was in Miami for a food demo this past January, my host Andrea G., knowing that I'm an ice cream fan, recommended that I stop by Serendipity.

I remember the anticipation, sitting in traffic while trying to get up Collins Avenue, from Miami Beach to Surfside, in the middle of the day.

But then I parked. And reached Serendipity. And ordered a scoop of Birthday Cake Ice Cream and a scoop of Cereal Milk Ice Cream. And the next thing I remember is feeling like wanting to dance on the sidewalk.

Owner Jessica Weiss was inspired to open Serendipity to fuel an obsession with nonfat frozen yogurt. This adorable shop is styled like the classic ice cream parlor and features tons of homemade hard ice cream flavors (they're *chalav Yisrael* too), which is made from scratch in small batches. The flavors are full of personality and are made using local and organic ingredients whenever possible.

You'll also find both sweet and tart nonfat frozen yogurt, and nondairy yogurt made from soymilk. Serendipity is also a coffee shop. If you're not ice cream obsessed, you can fuel your latte obsession (or both).

When Jessica shared this recipe, every taste was exactly as I remembered experiencing that day in Miami. It's worth buying an ice cream maker to bring a taste of Serendipity to your home. -V.

276

CEREAL MILK ICE CREAM

INGREDIENTS

2 CUPS	heavy cream
¾ CUP	sugar
•	pinch kosher salt
5 LARGE	egg yolks
3 CUPS	cornflakes
2 CUPS	whole milk
2 TBSP	light brown sugar

YIELD *1 quart*

CATEGORY *dairy*

DESCRIPTION

The ice cream version of the milk at the bottom of your cereal bowl

We garnished our ice cream with cornflake brittle. Simply caramelize sugar (see Techniques, page 13) and pour over cornflakes. Once caramel sets, break into chunks.

INSTRUCTIONS

1 In a medium saucepan over medium heat, warm the cream, sugar, and salt.

2 In a large bowl, whisk egg yolks. Slowly pour the warm cream into the yolks, whisking constantly as you pour. Transfer the mixture back to the pan and cook over low heat, stirring constantly, until custard thickens and coats the back of the spoon (See Techniques, page 12).

3 Strain the mixture into a bowl over an ice bath and let cool. Once cool, refrigerate for 4 hours.

4 Meanwhile, in a large bowl, combine cornflakes and milk. Let steep for 20 minutes. Use a strainer to remove as much of the cornflakes as possible. If cornflakes remain, you can repeat the process using cheesecloth. Discard soggy cornflakes. Add brown sugar to the milk. Set aside.

5 Once custard is cold, mix in cereal milk. Freeze the ice cream mix in your ice cream maker according to the manufacturer's instructions.

Entertaining? Fill mini Mason jars with your homemade ice cream. To serve, place the jars (with the lids) in a beverage tub filled with ice.

Perfect ice cream does take a little patience. Double the recipe so you always have some in the freezer. A double recipe fits perfectly in a 2-quart ice cream maker.

Once you buy your ice cream maker, always keep your ice cream bowl frozen so you can make ice cream without delay.

THE RESTAURANTS

UNITED STATES

ARIZONA

Segal's Oasis Grill
Phoenix, AZ
602.285.1515
www.segalsonestop.com/
oasis_grill.php

> Eggplant Chicken
> in Garlic Sauce
> *page 124*

> Slow-Cooked Okinawa Ribs
> *page 180*

CALIFORNIA

Bistro Natalie
Los Angeles, CA
310.246.1326
www.bistronatalie.com

> Bolognese
> *page 182*

Fish Grill
Los Angeles, CA

Beverly • 323.937.7162
Brentwood • 310.479.1800
Malibu • 310.456.8585
Pico • 310.860.1182
www.fishgrill.com

> Blackened Fish
> *page 202*

La Gondola
Beverly Hills, CA
310.247.1239
www.lagondola.com

> Beef Tinga Sliders
> *page 40*

Mexikosher
Los Angeles, CA
310.271.0900
www.mexikosher.com

> Huevos Motuleños
> *page 44*

Shiloh's
Los Angeles, CA
310.858.1652

> Ahi Tuna Two Ways
> *page 26*

Tierra Sur
Oxnard, CA
805.983.1560
www.tierrasuratherzog.com

> Zeppoli Cinnamon
> Doughnuts
> *page 266*

FLORIDA

Beyond by Shemtov's
Miami Beach, FL
305.538.2123
www.beyondbyshemtovs.com

> Salmon with
> Lemon & Caper Sauce
> *page 206*

Cine Citta
Surfside, FL
305.407.8319
www.cinecittamiami.com

> Fettuccine
> Tri Funghi
> *page 230*

> Chocolate Soufflé
> *page 270*

The Harbour Grill
Surfside, FL
305.861.0787
www.theharbourgrill.com

> Osso Buco
> *page 186*

Rare Hospitality
Miami Beach, FL
305.532.7273
www.raregroupmiami.com

> Heirloom Tomato Salad
> *page 102*

> Rare Bistro's "Crab" Cakes
> *page 209*

Serendipity Yogurt Café
Surfside, FL
305.865.1506

> Cereal Milk Ice Cream
> *page 276*

ILLINOIS

**Milt's Barbecue
for the Perplexed**
Chicago, IL
773.661.6384
www.miltsbbq.com

> Sweet Pickles
> *page 56*

Shallots Bistro
Skokie, IL
847.677.3463
www.shallotsbistro.com

> Chef's Special
> *page 164*

MASSACHUSETTS

Milk Street Café
Boston, MA
617.542.3663
www.milkstreetcafe.com

> Rockport Salad
> *page 118*

NEW JERSEY

Carlos & Gabby's
Lakewood, NJ
718.575.8226

> The Cedarhurst Sandwich
> *page 136*

Estréia
Lakewood, NJ
732.994.7878
www.estreia978.com

> Braised Short Ribs
> *page 156*

Etc. Steakhouse
Teaneck, NJ
201.357.5677
www.etcsteakhouse.com

> Honey-Mustard Hanger Steak
> *page 160*

Gotham Burger
Teaneck, NJ
201.530.7400
www.gothamburgerco.com

> Chicken Fingers +
> Cranberry BBQ Sauce
> *page 128*

Kosher Chinese Express
Manalapan, NJ
732.866.1677
www.kosherchinese88.com

> Sesame Chicken
> *page 148*

Mocha Bleu
Teaneck, NJ
201.837.2538
www.mochableu.com

> Sea Bass Spring Rolls
> *page 29*

Ottimo Café
Howell, NJ
732.367.0009
www.ottimocafe.com

> Tortelloni
> *page 216*

T Fusion Steakhouse
Brooklyn, NY
718. 62-STEAK
www.tfusionsteakhouse.com

   Bourbon BBQ Ribs
   page 172

The Upper Crust
Cedarhurst, New York
516.341.7211

   Taco Supreme Salad
   page 110

Wolf & Lamb Steakhouse
New York, NY • 212.317.1950
Brooklyn, NY • 718.627.4676
www.wolfandlambsteakhouse.com

   Crème Brûlée
   page 258

PENNSYLVANIA

Citron and Rose
Philadelphia, PA
610.664.4919
www.citronandrose.com

   Sweet Potato Soup
   page 72

CANADA

Java Café
Glencairn, Toronto
877.666.4101
www.omnijewelcrafters.com/java-cafe

   Portobello Mushroom Soup
   page 76

Pizza Pita
Montréal, QC
514.731.7482
www.pizzapita.com

   Poutine
   page 60

ENGLAND

Maxim
London
+44.20.8455.0664

   Cannelloni
   page 220

PIZAZA
London

Hendon • +44.20.8202.9911
Golders Green • +44.20.8455.4455
www.pizaza.com

   Pizaza Milkshakes
   page 244

SOYO
London
+44.20.8458.8788
www.so-yo.co.uk

   Quinoa and Spinach Salad
   page 160

ISRAEL

David Citadel
Jerusalem
+972.2.621.2121

   Caesar Salad
   page 87

Haroa Bacafé
Kfar Haro'eh
+972.4.625.1451

   Spinach Quiche
   page 240

Red Heifer Steakhouse
Jerusalem
+972.2.624.0504

   House Salad
   page 94

Ricotta
Har Hotzvim, Jerusalem
+972.2.587.0222
www.ricotta.rest-e.co.il

   Vegetable & Feta Cheese Focaccia
   page 236

Rimon Bistro
Jerusalem
1599.50.10.30
www.caferimon.co.il

   California Salad
   page 90

Rimon Café
Jerusalem
+972.2.633.3034
1599.50.10.30
www.caferimon.co.il

   Salmon & Tuna with Teriyaki Sauce
   page 194

SOYO Café
Jerusalem
+972.2.623.5421
www.soyo.co.il

   Rosé Pasta
   page 228

Trattoria Haba
Jerusalem
+972.2.623.3379

   Cauliflower & Chickpea Salad
   page 114

ITALY

Gam Gam Kosher Restaurant
Venice, Italy
+39.366.250.4505
www.gamgamkosher.com

   Eggplant Ghetto Style
   page 66

MEXICO

The Urban Grill
Mexico City, Mexico
+52.55.2167.5247
www.theurbangrill.mx

   Chermoula Chicken Breast
   page 144

PANAMA

Darna
Panama City, Panama
+507.302.2989
www.darna.com.pa
Darna's Bread Punta Pacifica
Darna's Bread Paitilla Mall
Darna's Bread Multicentro
Darna's Gourmet Boutique
Lula By Darna — Plaza Obarrio
(meat restaurant)
www.lulabydarna.com

   Darna's Salad
   page 84

INDEX

SOURCES:

HEREND *www.herendusa.com*
Page 19, 23, 76, 89, 107, 161

SET YOUR TABLE, *Lakewood, NJ and Monsey, NY* • 732.987.5569
Page 19, 23, 27, 41, 77, 89, 91, 103, 107, 153, 157, 161, 183, 199, 203, 207, 217, 221, 231, 245, 255

THE TABLE *by CS Thau*
732.363.2239
Page 23, 53, 73, 81, 91, 95, 107, 225, 259, 267

RENEE MULLER COLLECTION
www.reneemullerstyling.com
Page 31, 33, 65, 73, 99, 107, 137, 145, 169, 173, 191, 195, 237, 245

CB2 *www.cb2.com*
Page 49, 191, 267, 273

AMIT FARBER COLLECTION
www.shufunidesign.co.il
Page 67, 85, 133, 177, 181, 211, 229, 271

IKEA *www.ikea.com*
Page 73, 81, 95, 111, 119, 129, 145, 165, 225

SUR LA TABLE *www.surlatable.com*
Page 259